"There are few voices I trust more for clarity, guidance and wisdom than Rachel Gilson. In this book she enables parents to approach intimidating subjects with confidence and skill, taking advantage of the divinely orchestrated discipleship moments God supplies as we raise our children. Practical, faithful, discerning, insightful—Rachel is a gift to the church, and I love learning from her."

J.D. GREEAR, Pastor, The Summit Church, Raleigh-Durham, NC; Author, *Just Ask* and *Essential Christianity*

"In an age when we are called to be true to our inner selves, what you'll find in this book is exactly what's printed on the cover: *Parenting without Panic*. From one parent to another, Rachel offers real-world advice anchored in the eternal goodness and wisdom of the Bible. No angst, no rancour, but 'creating and testing our best practices right now' in light of God's promises to us in Jesus. An easily accessible and empowering read for every parent."

CRAIG ROBERTS, CEO, Sydney Anglican Youthworks

"Christian parents are in desperate need of Jesus-centered guidance as they talk to their kids about LGBT questions. This short book is just what we have all been waiting for: a master class in truth and love, equipping us to raise this generation with a cross-shaped understanding of discipleship and pointing them to Jesus' unending love as we explain the Bible's boundaries around sex and the goodness of how God has made our bodies."

REBECCA McLAUGHLIN, Author, *Confronting Christianity* and *Does the Bible Affirm Same-Sex Relationships?*

T0190695

"I hope that every Christian parent, teacher, pastor, counselor, or anyone else who ministers to children will take the time to read this short primer on preparing children to withstand, as disciples, the cultural affirmation of LGBT+ narratives, as well as what may be their own confusion. Rachel Gilson is both rock solid in affirming all God's commandments and will for male and female identities, while at the same time urging graciousness and kindness toward those who have adopted a broken understanding of sexuality. I would hope Christians would be moved to pass this small volume along to those who hold a different view from the Bible, in the hopes that they would learn that to disagree is not to hate and that the gospel of Jesus is our resource for all kinds of brokenness."

KATHY KELLER, Former Assistant Director of Communications, Redeemer Presbyterian Church, NYC; Coauthor, *The Meaning of Marriage*

"If you're like most Christian parents, you have been considering how to best address this generation's LGBTQ+ questions with your children. This topic intimidates and scares so many of us, but Rachel Gilson's new book is here to endow us with confidence so we can approach even the toughest questions with truth and grace rooted in Jesus and his word. This should be required reading for any and every Christian parent."

ADAM GRIFFIN, Lead Pastor, Eastside Community Church, Dallas, TX; Host, Family Discipleship Podcast

"*Parenting without Panic in an LGBT-Affirming World* can be welcomed by parents with a huge sigh of relief! Rachel writes as a true friend who understands what you are facing and as a brave ally who can help when your child needs support. Let's all thank her for her honesty, faithfulness, and wisdom."

RAY AND JANI ORTLUND, Renewal Ministries, Nashville, TN

"A marvellous little book that asks all the hardest questions about parenting and sexuality, and gives wise, loving, and thoughtful answers. Rachel has served us magnificently by thinking through how to raise children from toddlers to teenagers, without fear and without compromise. Superb."

ANDREW WILSON, Teaching Pastor, King's Church, London, UK; Co-author, *The Life You Never Expected*

"Rachel Gilson has written the book that Christian parents have been needing for some time—a book designed to equip us and our children to navigate faithfully LGBT+ questions and to do so, as she puts it, 'not as adversaries but as missionaries.' Clarity and a sense of reality characterize her writing. Most important of all, however, biblical truth and gospel grace permeate every page. When it comes to imparting the wisdom of God's ways to Christian children and preparing them for discipleship in an LGBT+-affirming world, this brief resource is the ideal place in which to begin."

ROB S. SMITH, Lecturer, Sydney Missionary Bible College, Sydney, Australia; Author, *How Should We Think about Gender and Identity?* and *The Body God Gives: A Biblical Response to Transgender Theory*

"A triumph of both calmness and confidence. To parents and all who love young people, Gilson models calmness in the presence of panic and confidence in the face of anxiety. But, even more importantly, she equips readers to rest calmly in God's steadfast faithfulness and confidently in his enduring goodness. This is a book which truly lives up to its title and is a blessing to all who seek to disciple children with Jesus' truth and love."

DANI TREWEEK, Founding Director, Single Minded Ministry; Author, *The Meaning of Singleness*

Rachel
Gilson

PARENTING

WITHOUT PANIC

IN AN LGBT
AFFIRMING
WORLD

thegoodbook
COMPANY

Parenting without Panic in an LGBT-Affirming World
© 2024 Rachel Gilson.

Published by:
The Good Book Company

thegoodbook.com | thegoodbook.co.uk
thegoodbook.com.au | thegoodbook.co.nz | thegoodbook.co.in

ISBN: 9781802541120 | JOB-007776 | Printed in the UK | Design by Drew McCall

CONTENTS

INTRODUCTION

"ALL OF THE KINDERGARTEN teachers are amazing—but did you know one is a woman who is married to another woman?"

My stomach sank when I heard Laura say this. I had just enrolled my daughter to start kindergarten in the neighborhood public school where Laura also sent two of her children. Like any parent, I had excitement and other big feelings as my daughter prepared to head off to school; this was brand new for our little family of three. Laura was a natural friend to turn to for advance news. But I truly hadn't expected that piece of information.

My first emotion was fear. My second emotion was shame.

My fear was instinctive, animal almost, not focused on one particular thing but as scattered as the toys lying all over my daughter's room.

As a follower of Jesus, what I want most for my daughter is for her to follow Jesus too. I want her to see him and what he says as good, true, and beautiful—

including what he says about our bodies, sex, and relationships. But what Jesus says about these topics is out of step with much of what the world now says. I knew I needed to prepare her, but kindergarten seemed impossibly early to start!

My daughter was only five years old. What could I say to her about this teacher that she would actually understand? Was it even age appropriate to talk about it? Her youth just made her so impressionable; I could imagine this teacher being warm, loving, and excellent—and without any effort at all showing my daughter that a woman being legally married to another woman was good.

Then there was the fear that if I tried to address the subject with my daughter, she would repeat it to her teacher or others at school in the least nuanced ways. We've all heard kids' interpretations of what they just heard from an adult. Let's just say they wouldn't be our first choice as ambassadors. What if she walked in and blurted, "MY mom said being gay is a SIN"? What kind of phone calls and meetings would I have to field? Would the school try to turn my daughter against me, persuading her that I was bigoted and wrong?

There was also a fear that her new little peers, if they knew what her family believed, would reject her, mock her, or perhaps shun her. Perhaps it wouldn't happen in kindergarten, but as all the kids advanced through school together, at some point it would become clear that our family was not in lock-step with our community on LGBT+ questions. Being from a committed Christian family can already make you seem strange. Would our very different views on sexuality cause too much social strain and make her want to walk away from faith? And what if she came to me with questions I just couldn't answer or with arguments for embracing LGBT+ identities and practices that I couldn't dissuade her from?

But even stronger than this rush of fears was my sense of shame. Why shame? Because I felt that I, of all people, should be able to handle this. First, I experience same-sex attraction; folks who identify as LGBT+ are not frightening to me because this is a road I've walked myself. I had started dating other young women in high school, and even though at that time no state in America had legalized gay marriage, I knew I wanted to marry a woman someday. This didn't pose any moral problems for me because I was an atheist and thought that all objections to gay relationships came from bigotry, stupidity, or both. During my first year at college, however, God interrupted my life. After stealing a copy of *Mere Christianity* by C.S. Lewis from a classmate, I was confronted with the gospel: that though I was a sinner deserving death, Jesus had come to absorb God's wrath towards me on the cross, to forgive me of my sin, and to give me, by his resurrection from the grave, a new life, now and forever. This news suddenly became the defining center of my life.

Which leads to the second reason why I felt shame. I've been thinking about, reading about, and writing about how to navigate LGBT+ questions as a Christian for decades. My same-sex attraction didn't simply disappear when I started following Jesus, and I had to work out what it meant to say "No" to those attractions and "Yes" to the Holy Spirit. That working out is the subject of my book *Born Again This Way*, as well as various articles I've written and talks I've given.

So shouldn't I, of all people, be equipped to help my own child navigate this scenario? Instead, I was thinking, "Please God, let her get one of the other two teachers; I'm not ready to handle this."

I don't know how you'd feel if you had been in my shoes. Maybe you would feel conflicted because you yourself still have questions about what the Bible says about sexuality. Or perhaps you feel secure in what the Bible teaches, but the postures of people who argue both for and against a traditional Christian perspective seem off-putting and uncomfortable to you—not much like the Jesus you encounter in Scripture—and you don't want to become one of them. No matter where you are personally, I know each of us have big questions and big emotions as we come to this topic and our kids.

I'm writing this little book for parents because I myself needed and need it. What's more, I know from my conversations at churches and conferences that I'm not the only one feeling these fears. We simply don't feel prepared to help our children navigate these questions because most of us aren't sure how to navigate them ourselves. If no one has equipped us first, how can we avoid being anything but the blind leading the blind, with both ourselves and our children ending up in a pit?

Our fears aren't baseless. So many of them make sense, given the facts on the ground and in our own lives. We don't gain anything by pretending our fears don't exist or by trying to shove them into the overstuffed junk drawer of our minds. At the same time, it is dangerous to feed these fears or to be ruled by them, "for God gave us a spirit not of fear but of power and love and self-control" (2 Timothy 1:7).

The problem with fear is that it makes us act less like Jesus, not more. Fear tends to make us isolate ourselves instead of connecting with others and loving them. Fear tends to make us go on the attack instead of dying to ourselves. Fear is very real and very powerful, but Christ our Savior is more real and more powerful. He calls us and our children to life to the full (John 10:10).

The goal of this book is to help you equip the kids in your life to navigate LGBT+ questions with the grace and truth of Jesus Christ. This is tricky to do because these questions just weren't being asked a couple of decades ago—at least not as frequently, as intensely, or as publicly as they are now. All of us are trying to figure out on the fly how to parent in this cultural moment. This means we're creating and testing our best practices right now. This is a vulnerable place to be, but we can be confident that we have been given what we need. God has graciously given us his word, his Spirit, and his people so that we can be faithful disciples in any generation, including this one.

This little book is for us—as parents, grandparents, aunts and uncles, and anyone who cares for children—by

God's grace, to move from a place of fear to one of humble confidence and faith. The chapters are therefore designed to lead with principles that can help us make that move, with some practical options for applying these principles at the end of each chapter.

We'll start by exploring God's positive vision for our bodies and relationships, which is the foundation for all that follows. After that, we'll discuss what it means to communicate these things to our kids in age-appropriate ways. Next, we'll think about how sin and brokenness impact God's good design. This will set us up to talk about useful tools for talking to our kids about LGBT+ questions. Then we'll be ready to tackle how to equip our kids to think about being Christians in a world that is rapidly changing. Finally, we'll consider how to respond when LGBT+ questions become personal for some of the children we love.

Each of our kids is unique. Each of our contexts is complex. There isn't a set script or roadmap tailor-made for us. But the Bible promises, "If any of you lacks wisdom, let him ask God, who gives generously to all without reproach, and it will be given him" (James 1:5). So, let us pray diligently and have grace with ourselves and each other as we seek to apply God's wisdom.

1

GOD'S POSITIVE VISION

THERE ISN'T ANYTHING QUITE like the power of "No." When dropped upon a child, it has explosive force. "No" to an extra show, a piece of candy, or more tablet time strikes children as a cruel injustice. They posture and protest as if the adult before them exists only to take pleasure in their pain: "But I WANT it!"

This frenzy of destructive energy is matched only when the child understands that she, too, can wield the power of "No." Vegetables? "No!" Sharing? "No!" Bedtime? "Double no!!" My friend has a young son who can get on such a "No" run that you can start offering him things he truly loves, and he'll just as fiercely scowl and repeat "No" at you.

As givers and as receivers, we have all experienced that "No" is sometimes necessary, yet often abused. And even when necessary, it can sting. It can be wielded without pity, without thought, without gentleness or understanding. Just this morning, tired and impatient, I snapped at my daughter that she is *not* to touch my phone unless given permission—and immediately knew that I could have communicated the same "No" in a better way.

When it comes to what the Bible says about sex, we may expect to hear an equally brutal "No." Growing up outside of church, my perception of Christianity's attitude towards sexuality could be summed up as backward, prudish, and oppressive. Unfortunately, many of my friends who *did* grow up going to church didn't have a much better experience. Some of my friends felt a tense contradiction on the topic. On the one hand, sexual desire was talked about like it could only ever be a destructive fire, leaving men and women scorched, bereft, and ashamed. On the other hand, they heard that they should get married as soon as possible so that they too could finally have sex. Other friends tell me that sex was a forbidden topic; instead of contradiction, there was silence.

One of the disconcerting things about being a parent is how often we find ourselves saying to our children the very things that our parents said to us. So if, with regards to sexuality, we were formed by the pervasive, frightening "No" that hovered around sex, we will need to be intentional about not simply transmitting that to our children. We first need to go back to the Bible to check whether what we learned is really the full-orbed vision of sex and sexuality that the Bible teaches.

I want to suggest that God's first words about our bodies and how to use them were not "No" but "Yes"— and that any place where he says "No" springs from this

"Yes" and is for our own good. I believe that if we grow more competent in expressing God's positive vision for sexuality to our children—if they have a chance to see what God is *for*, and only with this "Yes" in place to hear what God is against—then they will have a much better shot at experiencing and expressing the Bible's vision with grace and truth.

So, in this chapter we're going to look at the "Yes" God has said to our bodies, to marriage, and to singleness.

TRUST YOUR BODY

When my daughter was a toddler, I marveled at how many children's songs and stories existed solely to ensure that she knew the names and sounds of barnyard animals. I suppose there are still kids in America who regularly interact with cows, pigs, horses, goats, and the like, but my child, like many, is a city girl. She's seen way more squirrels and pigeons than roosters and hens, but no one is writing cute songs about what racoons sound like when they're digging through your trash. In any case, she soon became an expert at matching Moo to Cow and Oink to Pig. The overall theme was that you can trust the sound an animal makes to reveal what it is. You'll never hear a duck meowing or a cat trying to quack. Some things really just are what they are, and what is more, they *tell* you what they are.

Similarly, when it comes to sexuality, one place where we can and should start with our kids is simply this: they can trust their body to tell them who they are.

One of the beautiful truths of Christianity is that God calls creation good. Many religions today and in history have doubted this goodness because of the presence of brokenness and sin. And Christianity does not deny this brokenness. In fact, in chapter 3 we'll look at it squarely. (This is especially important for our kids who have disorders of sexual development—some of which are sometimes called intersex conditions—who need to know they are not cut off from God's goodness and love.)

Yet we know from Scripture that brokenness and troubles are not intrinsic to the project: that is, creation did exist in pure goodness and will someday again. In the creation story in Genesis 1, God repeatedly declares that the things he has made are good. Land and light: good. Water and air: good. Humanity, created in God's image, male and female: *very* good.

We don't need to have overly complex conversations with our kids about theories of sex and gender. The "very good" that God spoke over humanity as male and female establishes that we are called to receive the gift of our male or our female body as a good gift. Receiving it means that we are to live out, if we are male, our maleness identifiably as boys and men, and if we are female, our femaleness identifiably as girls and women (compare Deuteronomy 22:5; 1 Corinthians 11:2-16). From very early on, you can teach your children that their body shows them whether they are a male or a female, and therefore that they are a boy or a girl, and that being a boy or a girl is very good. It is so simple—something easily taken for granted—and yet the truth of a good God creating boys and girls, men and women, out of his love and for our joy is one of the most solid foundations we can give.

We can also point our kids to Jesus, who took on real humanity. He was born with the real body of a baby boy, born from the real body of a woman, showing the dignity and goodness of both. When he rose from the dead, he appeared to his disciples in a new body—but still a *human* body, which could be touched and seen and recognized as his. He wasn't just pretending to take on humanity or pretending to have body; it was and is real. We can teach our children that they have much dignity because they have a human body and soul, and that they can trust their body to show them who they are when it comes to being a boy or a girl, rather than questioning how much their feelings or interests line up with male or female stereotypes.

When they're little and in the bath, as we make sure each part is clean, we can teach them to be thankful for each part of their body because it is a good gift from God. When a new baby is born at church, we can remind our kids that that little one's tiny body tells us whether they are a girl or a boy, and that the gift of a brand new human is something to celebrate because God made humans good. As we run around outside, jumping and playing, we can thank God for good bodies that are powerful and bring joy. At Easter time we can tell our kids that Jesus purchased salvation not just for our souls but also for our male and female bodies forever. Bodies aren't a temporary gift but something we will enjoy for eternity.

SIGNPOSTS TO GOD'S GOODNESS

We also have good news to tell our kids about singleness and marriage. According to the Bible, both of these ways of living can communicate the goodness of the real Marriage between God and his people, Christ and his church. In addition to being able to trust that their bodies can tell them who they are, our children can learn how relationships are signposts that point to the goodness of God's forever family.

One beautiful thing about these signposts is that we can begin to talk about them with theological depth even to our very little children, long before we talk explicitly about sexuality. They are an image that can grow with our children and work in stages, setting up the later conversations.

SINGLENESS AS SIGNPOST

Let's start with a brief look at singleness. In our culture, both outside the church and inside, singleness can be portrayed as if it is one of the saddest ways to live if it lingers "too long." No one wonders with concern about the 22-year-old single; the same can't usually be said about the 42-year-old single. We can easily speak and act as if a person only really becomes whole or fulfilled or a grown-up once they have a romantic partner. The problem with this vision is that it's unbiblical and untrue.

When the Bible talks about the community God is creating—the church of Jesus Christ—it consistently uses the language of family. We are both "born again" into the family (John 3:3) and also adopted (Ephesians 1:5)! We become brothers and sisters one to another. Though we may leave father, mother, siblings and lands when we seek the kingdom of God, Jesus says that we gain them in much more abundance (with persecutions, he adds, in Mark 10:29-31).

What is inescapable about the biblical vision is that when a person is in Christ, they are also in his family. To be a Christian is to be in relationships—relationships that are to be marked with the intimacy, fellowship, and joy of a healthy family. A person's marital status does not determine whether they are in the family.

What's more, according to Jesus, in the new heavens and the new earth, all of us will be single. We discover this when Jesus, in a debate with religious leaders, teaches that there will be no human marriage in heaven (Matthew 22:29-30). But while the human spousal relationship will not endure, our relationship to each other as siblings will remain. This family is more fundamental than any other relationship. Single Christians radically demonstrate to the watching world that God's family is more inclusive and expansive than what the world has to offer, and it is forever. They are a signpost that the gospel isn't first about "No" but about the "Yes" of love relationships and mutual self-giving.

The New Testament dignifies singleness that is lived in purity and love. One way you can teach this to your children is in the way you speak to them about their future. You could choose to say, "if you get married" to your kids instead of "when you get married," for example. You can talk about how the family of God, which glorifies him as a good Father, is a gospel picture, and how one of our best gifts as disciples is to participate in and build up this family, the church. This helps everyone see how God's family unit, because it is forever, gets pride of place, and helps your kids know that they will always have a place in it through Christ. You can value your siblings in Christ, celebrating and mourning with them as the family they are, instead of reserving these things for biological or legal family. At our church, several families host Thanksgiving and Easter dinners where there are more church-family members than legal family members. I regularly talk with my daughter about how her church friends truly are her siblings, and I've seen this reflected in how she now talks about them as well.

So, singles who are thriving in the local church are a signpost to the boundary-shattering, good-news eternal family that God is creating through Christ. All of us, married or single, are responsible for making other members of our spiritual family feel valued and included. Single Christians will be in a position to thrive if they take this seriously. In a culture that believes in salvation-by-romance—that we are not full or real persons until we have a partner—a commitment to joyful participation in the family of God is a powerful vision of salvation by faith in Christ alone. This is what our kids need to hear and see, not the false gospel that they are worthless unless someone romantically loves them.

Faithful singleness plays another key role: it is a signpost to the real Marriage between Jesus and his church, which will be consummated when Jesus comes again (Revelation 19 – 21). A disciple living faithfully in singleness can say of human marriage, "That is a good and worthy thing, and even if I am not experiencing it now, I won't miss out on the real thing." A single person can declare with their very life that the resurrection is real, and really coming, and will be better than any earthly romance. This is an incredibly countercultural proclamation of the sweetness of the gospel in a society drunk on romance.

MARRIAGE AS SIGNPOST

Over and over in Scripture, God describes his relationship with his people using the picture of marriage. It's not the only picture God uses of course; the love between friends is also a gospel picture, as is the love of a mother for her child, and on and on. Nonetheless, marriage is one of God's favorite gospel pictures. Over and over we see God portrayed as a faithful, loving Husband and his people called to be a faithful, loving Bride. The picture is present in many places in the Bible, with some of the more famous examples occurring in Hosea and Isaiah, but the foremost is Ephesians 5:22-33, where Paul writes, "Husbands, love your wives, as Christ loved the church and gave himself up for her" (v 25) and "As the church submits to Christ, so also wives should submit in everything to their husbands" (v 24).

Now, God didn't look at human marriage and think, "Wow, that sort of reminds me of my relationship to my people." No! Marriage was designed from the outset to be a model—imperfect and miniature but true—of the real Marriage. So human marriage, if conducted in purity and love, can be a beautiful display of God's relationship with his people: a living, breathing picture of the gospel. This is something you can share with your kids over and over.

Why are husbands and wives called to be faithful throughout their whole lives? Because God is always faithful to his people, and his people are called to faithful love in return. Why do husbands and wives give birth to children and seek to bring children into their homes through adoption? Because God's relationship with his people is a fruitful family—a network of expansive love. Why are husbands and wives to give their bodies only to each other, in safety and joy? Because God's relationship with his people is exclusive: a place of true shelter and intimate love.

And why does the Bible speak of marriage exclusively as between a man and a woman, not two men or two women? Because God's love for his people and their love for him is a love across difference—not one between two interchangeable parties. Jesus and the church are not the same! And though there are many beautiful forms of human difference in the world, none is as fundamental as the original difference of male and female—a difference that registers even at the cellular level. And it is this special instance of diversity in unity—a male and female united in marriage—that is constantly employed in the Bible as a picture of God's relationship with his people.

As Paul explains in his letter to the Ephesians, since Jesus and his people play different roles in their love relationship, so husbands and wives are called to different roles in their love relationship. The spouses tell the gospel story by playing their assigned part: husbands loving their wives as Christ loves the church, and wives submitting to husbands as the church submits to Christ (Ephesians 5:22-33). Editing the story so that there are two people representing Christ, or two people representing the church, distorts the gospel picture just as deeply as the distortion of adultery, or the distortion of sexual violence in marriage. To these distortions and more, God says "No" because they are sin against his great "Yes" in Christ.

Yet when a marriage is undertaken by disciples of Christ in purity and love, it can show in its own small way a glimmer of what the gospel is. It is a signpost towards the ultimate Marriage between Jesus and his Bride, which will be consummated at the end (Revelation 19:7; 21:9-10).

In the promised new creation, all of us will be single, and all of us will participate in the Marriage, making up the Bride of Christ. That means that local churches now, if filled with healthy marriages and healthy singles, will have multiple powerful ways of pointing to that gospel vision. Our neighbors are longing for intimacy, for romance, and for connection, but they are being sold a cheap, plastic imitation of the real thing by the world around them. Only in Christ—where sin is forgiven, where transformation is available, where love that conquers death is promised—can this longing be met. It is what we need; it is what our children need; it is what our neighbors and the world need.

Every time something in our life exalts romance, we can talk to our kids about how that desire is met in the marriage of God with his people. Every time a story celebrates belonging and family, we can tell our kids about God's design for us to have these things, and how he is providing them first in his church. Every time our culture tells a story that singleness is dangerous or sad, we can tell our children of our single Savior, who proved that humans don't need mere romance to live well; we have all we need in God and in his people to thrive.

If our children hear again and again the ways that these things positively point to the gospel, they will become fluent in the *why* of God's sexual ethic. This will ease their understanding of the various "No's" that God says. But before we can move any farther, we need to talk about equipping our kids not just with theology but biology. We can't have full conversations about LGBT+ questions without laying the groundwork of physical bodies and reproduction, which we will turn to next.

KEY PRINCIPLES

▲ God created us male and female, and we can trust our bodies to tell us who we are: boys or girls, men or women.

◡ God created marriage and singleness to tell the story of the gospel. Both of these ways to live can be joyful, fruitful, and fulfilling in God's family.

PRACTICES FOR PARENTING

● Look for everyday examples and opportunities to teach about the goodness of our bodies and to reinforce the goodness of humanity's creation as male and female. Think creatively about bath time, the birth of babies, playtime, and more as ways of celebrating bodies and the male/female distinction.

▪ Similarly, make frequent mentions of how singleness and marriage both tell the gospel. As you watch movies, listen to songs, and enjoy your single and married friends, remind your kids about the gospel picture present in these places.

▲ Teach your children about the family of God: how believers are all sons and daughters of our Father in heaven and therefore brothers and sisters to one another. Practice valuing your local church family with your kids: invite different kinds of people over for a chaotic family meal and bedtime or together attend an event of importance in a church friend's life, such as a birthday party.

2

SEX TALK

WHEN I PICKED MY daughter up from kindergarten one early spring day, she told me very matter of factly, "My teacher said her wife is pregnant." I'm pretty sure I said something profound like "Oh!" My daughter continued, sort of musing to herself, "But it's not possible for my teacher and her wife to have a baby by themselves, so I wonder what they did about that."

I was struck and relieved by her tone. She wasn't sneering about her teacher or afraid or confused. I was also pleased to see that my attempts to explain conception to her, piecemeal over the past couple of years, had produced a practical knowledge that gave her an ability to reflect on her teacher's situation.

I started explaining reproduction to my daughter when she was around the tender age of three, if not before (the details of life with a toddler are fuzzy for me, considering how exhausting those years were). And in this chapter, I want to help build your confidence that you both can and should talk about sex with your children earlier than you may have thought.

This might be very different from your own experience of learning about sex. I didn't grow up in the church, so I've had to gather the basic patterns of growing up evangelical (at least in America) by talking to my friends. I feel sort of like an old school anthropologist, equipped with field hat and notebook, transcribing rituals quite foreign to me. One of the most common stories I've heard is how "the talk" was handled. It appears that many people were given some sort of embarrassing book by their parents as they were in the process of puberty, and then either never talked about it again or had one excruciating conversation in a very formal setting. I'm sure experiences vary on how well this technique worked in producing a healthy and holy relationship to sexuality. But this approach is exactly the wrong one if we want to help our kids navigate LGBT+ questions well. This is not to heap blame on our parents, who were probably doing their best with what they'd been taught. But with the support of God's word, God's people, and God's Spirit, we can give to our kids much better than many of us got.

CONSIDERING WHY

For most of us, the idea of talking to our kids openly and honestly about sexuality is about as appealing as walking into traffic blindfolded. We worry that we'll mess it up. We worry that we'll expose our kids too early to such an adult topic. We worry that we will get embarrassed and flustered. The only way to overcome these powerful deterrents is to recognize that talking to our kids about sex early will actually help them in the long run. Here are three reasons why I'm convinced of this.

One reason is that equipping our kids with basic biology helps to protect them from sexual abuse. Horrifically, some adults prey on children's ignorance, fear, and confusion in order to gain access to a child's body and keep their own abuse from being discovered. A child who doesn't know the proper names of their genitalia, or that certain body parts are to be kept private, is less likely to be able to understand or report what is happening to them. I desperately wish this were not my number 1 reason. But giving our kids some understanding that no one should be touching them in certain areas or asking them to touch them in certain areas is an important piece of protecting our kids against abuse and equipping them to report inappropriate requests or behaviors.

Related to this, a second reason for talking to our kids about sex early is that we want our children to know that we are trustworthy experts when it comes to sexuality. If we are the first ones to communicate to our kids about sex, and if we're able to do it with calm confidence—without shame or silliness—then our kids will be more able to tell us if they see or hear something that contradicts what they've heard from us. Even apart from abuse, children live in a social world. We never know when our sheltered seven-year-old might rub shoulders in children's church with a seven-year-old who has a 17-year-old brother who talks quite a lot about teenage things in front of his younger sibling. Additionally, if our children go to school, it is important for us to seek out information about what they are being taught and when. It may well be that certain topics are now taught earlier or in more detail than they were when we were young—and covering them with our children at home, *before* they learn them at school, is essential.

The world is confused and confusing when it comes to sexuality, before we even get to LGBT+ questions. Is sex something cheap and fun that you can do to make yourself feel good and that won't hurt anybody? Or is it something serious, meaningful, and powerful—so much so that you have to make sure to engage in it in order to be a real grown-up? Or is it neither, or both, of those things? As Christians, we know that the various stories that our society tells and believes about sexuality are scrambled and scrambling. There is simply no way to completely seal off our kids from these messages. And even if we could in childhood, Jesus Christ's vision for our children is that they would grow up to be disciples who are in the world but not of it (see John 17:14-16). We have a huge role in preparing them for that life of discipleship that we pray they will embrace.

If our children know that Mom and Dad tell them the truth about sex—that we know about sex and aren't embarrassed about it—our kids can have confidence to come to us with questions and to check the messages they hear against what they already have established from us. As scary as it can be to imagine having these conversations, it is better for our children to hear about sexuality for the first time from people who know them, love them, and want the very best for them, than from anyone else.

This brings up a third reason to have conversations early: we're not just mindful of protecting our children; we also want them to be able to rejoice in and embrace God's positive vision for sexuality, which was laid out in chapter 1. No one can live off of a diet of "No"; we're fed and nurtured on "Yes." Now, that doesn't mean your toddler needs a master's seminar on human sexuality. But a life of "Yes" is built on a solid foundation laid by parents and other trusted adults. And this "Yes" is what helps our kids think through with discernment any stance on sexuality that falls outside of God's design. Brick by age-appropriate brick, we can give our kids something sturdy, true, and even beautiful.

CONSIDERING HOW

With all the places where a person could start, one of the best is simply to teach vocabulary. We know this even from the way we teach our children deep, complex ideas from our Christian faith. We don't expect our toddlers to articulate a doctrine of the Trinity, but we teach them the names of the three Persons in the one true and living God: the Father, the Son, and the Holy Spirit. We don't get into the nitty-gritty of atonement theories with our kindergarten students, but in order to tell them the wonderful news of the gospel, they need specific words like *cross, sin, salvation, forgiveness*.

So too with sexuality: we need first to give our children the right words. All kids can and should have access to the real names of their body parts. When it comes to sexuality, the very first brick your children need for the foundation is that a male has a penis and a female has a vagina.

Some of us grew up using very silly words for genitalia. Others of us grew up with vaginas and penises never being mentioned at all; that area of our body was mentioned vaguely or never. Some of us still feel uncomfortable saying "penis" or "vagina" even in a medical setting. But these words are not inappropriate, and our children need them. Are you alone right now, reading? You could practice right this second just saying "vagina" and "penis" out loud. Maybe it will feel especially strange; but we have a much better chance of being able to teach these words to our kids if we've practiced them. If we can communicate with a calm and confident tone, "That is your penis" and "This is your vagina," our kids will receive our expertise and absorb that they don't need to be afraid or ashamed of the bodies God gave them.

If teaching "vagina" and "penis" constitutes Round 1—the body parts one can see—Round 2 vocabulary moves to words describing things our children can't see but which are vital in explaining sexuality. These words are "seed" and "egg."

The question of when to introduce these terms, which are less obvious than "penis" and "vagina," has to do with when your kids naturally start asking about babies and pregnancy. My daughter was one of those kids who was fascinated with babies and just started asking about them at a young age. I had literally no idea what to do but assumed that telling her the biological basics was probably a good foundation. For basic biology, that means sperm and egg coming together, but when I considered those terms, I was conflicted. "Egg" was a concept my daughter already knew, but "sperm" seemed to invite more problems than it solved. Being a Bible nerd, I thought "seed" worked just as well; this is the word used throughout the Bible in promises related to offspring, as in Genesis 22:18, when God promises to Abraham, "In your offspring [seed, compare KJV] shall all the nations of the earth be blessed." And my daughter could see other types of seeds, just as she could see other types of eggs.

I recently learned that a great program for teaching parents to talk to their little kids about sex, called Birds and Bees, also uses the language of seeds and eggs for teaching the basics.[1] This was a huge relief to me, since I was definitely winging it. I was introduced to Birds and Bees by my friend Julie, mother of four, and having listened to these materials, I highly recommend them.

They recommend that we don't jump right in with human reproduction, but instead we instill a fascination in our kids with the way things grow. I love this advice because it reminds us that while we humans are made "a little lower than the heavenly beings" (Psalm 8:5), we are also people of the dust (Genesis 3:19)—one type of creature among many. God designed life to reproduce in certain ways, and we're part of that.

---

1 https://birds-bees.com/

Frankly, in most societies throughout history, families lived with and around animals all the time. You needed cows for milk, chickens for your eggs, and so on. It wouldn't take long for children to learn where new cows came from because they would be living among them. But here we are, in apartments instead of on farms, with spayed and neutered house pets. We need the extra help.

Your child may be familiar with plant seeds and how the seed of a green bean planted will, with water and light, produce a new green-bean plant. We can then explain that for animals, we need a seed and an egg to come together. For animals, seeds alone don't produce new life, and neither do eggs alone. Puppies come from the seeds and eggs of dogs coming together; piglets come from the seeds and eggs of pigs coming together.

This means that when we get to talking about where human babies come from, we've laid the foundation; they come from a human seed and a human egg coming together.

Plenty of us have kids who ask lots of questions, but others don't. Another tip I loved from the Birds and Bees program was that some of our kids just aren't question-askers, and yet they also need to know about reproduction. Birds and Bees have a lovely phrase: "Have you ever wondered...?" So you can ask your child, "Hey, have you ever wondered where babies come from? Well, it's pretty amazing, let me tell you." You could try this first with baby animals and work up to human babies.

Whether you have a questioner or not, these conversations about penises and vaginas, seeds and eggs, are not a one-and-done deal. Again, this is just the same as how we teach our kids about the gospel. We don't simply explain Jesus' death on the cross one time and then never revisit it. No, because it's the most important good news our kids can hear, we talk early and often about the basics of the Christian faith. We know that we and our kids need to hear the gospel a lot to really internalize it and to correct misunderstandings that may have snuck in along the way. The principle with sexuality is similar. Little by little, we want to answer our kids' questions, use the right vocabulary, and develop in them a delight in and knowledge of the beautiful process of new life. They won't get all they need in just one conversation.

THE SEX TALK

But let's be honest: no amount of identifying penises and vaginas, or discussing seeds and eggs, will let you off the hook for explaining how *that* human seed gets to *that* human egg.

Again, I so appreciated the wisdom with which the Birds and Bees curriculum discussed this aspect of the conversation; I can't recommend enough their approach on talking to kids about conception. They offered many things, but one reminder and one piece of practical advice really stood out.

The reminder was that when we think or talk about sex, we are adults. We have baggage, history, and all kinds of emotions about sexuality that we bring to the table. This includes the fact that having gone through puberty, we are sexualized beings in a way that small children are not. This is another great reason to talk to our kids early: they don't have this baggage, and they don't relate to the sex act in the same way. For example, we might worry that just talking about biological processes could cause them to start feeling sexual desire. Honestly, they're most likely to hear the details and think, "Ew, I would never do that!"

The piece of advice was an actual script for telling children how conception happens. If you haven't had the seed-and-egg discussion, or if it's been a while, you can begin by reminding your child that when a seed meets an egg, that's the beginning of a new baby's life. And then the description: "The husband places his penis inside his wife's vagina. Then the seed travels through the penis to get to the egg inside the wife."

Take a deep breath. Drink a glass of water. But more than anything, practice the sentence. It is so helpful to not go it alone in this moment but to have a prepared phrase—and this one has so much to commend it. First, it is explicit about husbands and wives, teaching that there is a right context and commitment for this act. Second, it is biological and medical and completely accurate, yet without getting into details that children don't need. Third, it shows the complementary nature of the male and female bodies, the necessity of both, and their dignity in participating in the creation of new life. Of course, it doesn't say everything; much later kids can come to understand that sexual connection isn't merely for conception, that infertility is real, and that males and females are more than just their reproductive design. We all know that there is so much more to sexuality than those two sentences. And yet, for the task at hand, those sentences serve beautifully.

Once you have laid this foundation, you can return to it as needed, and you will need to. Very embarrassingly (for me), I had my daughter ask me in the car, months after I had first explained how the seed got to the egg, if I had to swallow the seed for it to get to the egg. Who even knows what my face looked like. But by God's grace I was able to calmly explain that, no, because babies don't grow in tummies, the seed can't get to the egg in the way food gets to the stomach. Babies grow in wombs, and the seed gets to the egg in the womb by traveling through the husband's penis, which is placed inside his wife's vagina, because the vagina leads to the womb. She said something like, "Oh yeah, that makes sense," and, besides a very red face on my part, everyone was fine.

If you practice speaking with calm confidence, your kids will feel that you are the expert. You can tell them that if they ever hear something different or confusing about sexuality, they can come to you, and you will tell them the truth.

HOW DOES THIS RELATE TO LGBT+ QUESTIONS?

Giving our kids a clear, honest description of God's design for sexuality in its physiological aspects is a crucial component to having healthy conversations about LGBT+ questions. While I think the theological picture we explored in chapter 1 is even more important, we simply can't ignore the importance of talking about the biology too.

If we give our children the correct vocabulary for genitalia, it reinforces the given order of male and female. Boys and men have penises; girls and women have vaginas. God made male and female very good, and while genitals are not the only signal of sex, they are a reliable one. In a world which says that gender is based on an internal feeling, establishing the outward facts about our bodies is a rock solid foundation on which you can later build. The earlier we give our children the correct words for body parts, and the earlier we establish ourselves as experts they can trust, the better they will be able to rest on the goodness of God's design.

If we give our children the age-appropriate medical knowledge of how conception works, they will be equipped to understand that male and female bodies unite to produce new life—something distinct and beautiful. This supports the theological truth that God's relationship with his people is fruitful, bringing life where there was none, which is part of how marriage is a picture of the gospel. It can produce a foundation based on which our children know that seed and seed alone, or egg and egg alone, have no power in this way. I don't think that this fact on its own can overcome the strong messaging for approval of same-sex romantic and sexual relationships that our children will hear, but I do think that the facts of biology as created and given by God reveal his order in vivid and powerful ways.

An early understanding that our loving and wise God created all these things equips our children to see that while the world uses sexuality in all kinds of ways, only certain uses are blessed by God and produce his good, gospel fruit.

Having established that, there are more concrete conversations that we'll need to have with our kids about LGBT+ questions. We'll consider those in chapter 4—but before we do that, we need to briefly explore another deeply important theological conversation: how sin has impacted God's good design.

KEY PRINCIPLES

▲ You are the best first teacher of your child when it comes to learning about reproduction; be wise and courageous about taking up this task.

〰 Teaching children the correct names of their body parts, as well as how reproduction works, helps keep them safe and gives them a strong foundation for healthy, biblical sexuality.

PRACTICES FOR PARENTING

● Look for ways to talk about how God designed new animal life to begin: always with a seed and an egg. Lots of little-kid books and shows focus on baby animals, which is a great entry point.

〰 Use the correct terms for your child's body and other bodies; it is good for your kids to know that males have penises and females have vaginas.

- Practice these sentences: "The husband places his penis inside his wife's vagina. Then the seed travels through the penis to get to the egg inside the wife."

  - Your child may ask you something like "But how does the seed get to the egg?" Or "How does the baby get inside the mommy?"

  - And you have practiced for this moment! You're ready!

  - You can then say, "I'm so glad you asked. This is a great question. It's amazing how God designed it. How it happens is, the husband places his penis inside his wife's vagina. Then the seed travels through the penis to get to the egg inside the wife."

▲ It is never too late to start these principles. Even if you haven't used the correct terms before, or talked about these things early with your child, you can start now. It is so important your child knows that you are a safe and knowledgeable person to come to with questions about bodies and sexuality.

3

THE IMPACT OF
THE FALL

I WAS TRICKED INTO moving to New England by savvy college advertising. It was all about the fall. As a Californian, I found the photos of students enjoying college life amid vibrant red, orange, and yellow trees intoxicating. The pamphlets made it seem that it was perpetually fall on campus, and I was hooked. Having lived here for several decades since college, I can confirm that fall in New England really is amazing—chock-full of cider, donuts, pumpkins, and, yes, those beautiful leaves.

Unfortunately, when we come to the Bible, the Fall means something else entirely: not the time when everything is just right but when everything went wrong.

So far we've seen that God has a positive vision for our bodies, for singleness, and for marriage, and how talking to our kids early about their bodies and reproduction helps reinforce this good design. But it doesn't take long for us to realize that we don't experience our bodies or relationships in an uncomplicated way. And especially as our children get older and are exposed to LGBT+ questions, we observe that not everyone seems to know about or care about God's good design, and not everything seems to line up with it. We need to disciple our children with these realities in mind, so that we can best prepare them to engage with these questions with Jesus' truth and love. First, in this chapter, we'll discuss the theological concepts, and in the following chapters, we'll consider how to relate these to our children, especially as they get older.

SIN AND BROKENNESS

The Fall is a word to describe the sin and brokenness that entered the world and all of us because of the sin of our first parents.

There are two dynamics at play here. Most of us are probably familiar with the word "sin," which describes the wrongdoing and wrong-feeling that infects us all—as individuals and collectively—and for which we are responsible. "Brokenness" or "fallenness" refers to how the sin of our first parents has fractured creation (including humanity)—like cracks in a beautiful piece of pottery—in ways that cause us to suffer and yet aren't an individual's fault.

Sin and brokenness were not part of God's original good creation; they entered later because of humanity's rebellion. And they will not be part of God's future restored creation either. One day, God will remove sin and its consequences permanently. But here and now, we all live with this sickness in us—a congenital defect from birth. We sin because we are sinners—actively rejecting God's loving rule in our lives. We suffer because we are broken—people with imperfect minds and bodies living in a beautiful world that is busted up too.

We see both of the categories at play in the story where Jesus met a man who had been blind since birth. Jesus was asked, "Who sinned, this man or his parents, that he was born blind?" Jesus answered, "It was not that this man sinned, or his parents" (John 9:3a). The man wasn't born blind due to some sin of his parents but because of the general fallenness caused by Adam and Eve's sin (and so that "the works of God might be displayed in him"). Of course, the man could have sinned in response to his brokenness. He could have cursed God for allowing the blindness to happen to him, for example. We often sin in response to brokenness, in fact, because we are sinners. We can have a condition of brokenness in our minds and bodies and also a sinful response to that brokenness in our hearts.

Both of these categories can be helpful with LGBT+ questions, and you don't need to be an expert in order to begin to use them with your kids. Here are some places in which to start.

First, we can help our kids understand that, as Christians, we expect things to go wrong with our minds and bodies. Brokenness impacts all of us, at the very least through the process of getting old and frail. We help our children when we recognize that there isn't a certain class of people whose bodies have been impacted. It's all of us, in one way or another. Similarly, we teach our children that all of us have been born rebels. We are not fundamentally good people who sometimes sin. We all sin because we all want to sin, because we are sinners.

The brokenness and sin that humanity ushered in with the Fall complicates our relationship with God's good design. Brokenness, for example, often means that we can't recognize the design fully because things in the world are damaged. And sin means that our hearts crave rebellion against God, and we act on these cravings. There are no bigger problems that face humanity than these. Only the death and resurrection of Jesus Christ, the perfect God-man, was sufficient to forgive our sin, to bring us healing and life, and to win creation's future renewal.

If we approach LGBT+ questions as if brokenness and sin is only *out there* and not first in ourselves, we will tell a lie. We need the gospel first ourselves. But our neighbors also need it. The complexity of brokenness and sin means that many around us are eager to affirm gay relationships and transgender identities. Armed with a positive vision for sexuality and an understanding of the Fall, we can better help our kids understand and respond biblically. First, we'll consider transgender identities; then we'll talk about disorders of sexual development; and finally we'll turn to same-sex attraction and gay relationships.

TRANSGENDER IDENTITIES

One of the challenges when it comes to equipping our kids to think biblically about transgender identities is that the culture around us is moving so fast, we can feel as if we're trying to board a train that's already moving. But it's worth establishing some basic starting points. Broadly speaking, when a male chooses to live in the world not as a boy or as a man, or when a female chooses to live in the world not as a girl or as a woman, most probably they have taken on a transgender identity. They may want people to identify them as the gender "opposite" to their biological sex (for example, a man who wants to be identified as a woman). Or they may want to identify in a gender category not attached to a particular sex, such as "non-binary" or "gender fluid." Even in these few sentences, we can feel how complex this all is, and we can easily feel overwhelmed ourselves, even before we try to talk to our children about it.

Thankfully, the truths of God's positive design combined with the Fall give us lots of tools to understand the various different reasons why a person might choose to adopt a transgender identity.

Some people may choose a transgender identity in response to gender dysphoria. This is an experience that varies widely but includes discomfort with and even a feeling of alienation from the body someone was born with. As Christians, we are not surprised when bodies aren't experienced as they were designed to be, because we know about the Fall! We can recognize that the experience of gender dysphoria is real without affirming that adopting a transgender identity is right.

It's also helpful to know that some people adopt a transgender identity for reasons apart from gender dysphoria. For example, sometimes it seems to them a proper response to sexism: the constant battle throughout history between the sexes can make some people think that perhaps the best fix is ditching the categories all together. As Christians we are not surprised by the sin of sexism. We see it in Genesis 3 itself.

We observe, then, that many people adopt transgender identities in response to real problems: problems with how they feel about their bodies and problems with how people relate to one another. As Christians, we can agree that these are problems! We can understand why people made in God's image would seek solutions to problems. We also, though, understand that because we are born rebels, who seek solutions in ourselves instead of in God, our answers will never meet the challenges that the problems pose. Trying to live in opposition to how God made our bodies cannot bring lasting peace. We can have understanding and compassion regarding the problems, while insisting that the gospel itself is what promises resolution.

God came as a man, born of a woman, to redeem humanity, both male and female. That doesn't mean that accepting Jesus as Lord and Savior makes sexism instantly go away or gender dysphoria evaporate. As Christians we know that brokenness and even sin remain until the day when Jesus will return. But it does mean that in Christ, we're enabled to accept the gift of our bodies and work for the dignity of all.

What's more, Christ promises to return and give his people brand new bodies as part of the new heavens and the new earth—which, for those with gender dysphoria, means a body in which they will finally feel at home, if they trust in Christ. No one else can do that, but it is a promise for all who come to him.

This is good news we can give to our children. They can trust their bodies, and they can trust that God made humanity male and female in his image, and that even when brokenness and sin touch these truths, Jesus is more powerful and promises restoration.

These truths could come out in our parenting in a number of ways. Sometimes, for example, we might be watching older movies or shows that have stereotypes about men or women. We can be attentive to what these stories communicate about women and men, and emphasize that one-dimensional portrayals don't communicate the same vision as that which God has for us. Our kids need to know that they don't have to be defined by stereotypes. If we have a son who likes art more than sport or a daughter who wants to be a firefighter when she grows up, we don't need to stamp that out of them. As it happens, I love watching American football and can't cook, while my husband enjoys cooking and doesn't care about men on a screen running up and down fields. But this doesn't make us any less a woman and a man! We can trust our bodies to tell us and our children whether we're male or female.

For some people, however, it's their bodies that are raising questions. So let's consider that next.

DISORDERS OF SEXUAL DEVELOPMENT / INTERSEX CONDITIONS

We've seen that the Fall has impacted all creation and human bodies in difficult ways, meaning that things don't always work according to design. Every human body is fallen because of the sin that humanity chose. But some people are born with particular physical challenges. For example, I know a child who was born without parts of his inner ear, meaning that without the help of a hearing aid, his ear won't function as it should. No doubt you know someone who was born with a disability or physical challenge of some kind—or you may have been born with a physical challenge yourself. Christians aren't surprised that these things happen. As Jesus made clear, they are not the result of some sin committed on the part of the baby or the parents. They are a more general consequence of the Fall.

Just as a baby can be born with a disorder in their hearing, so a child can be born with something disrupting normal sexual development. This is relatively rare: occurring in approximately 1 in 2,000 newborns.[2] Just as there are multiple kinds of hearing problems, some more serious than others, so there are multiple kinds of disorders of sexual development (some of which are called intersex conditions). Many of these conditions don't impact the ability to determine if a person is a male or a

---

2 "Disorders of Sexual Development: Current Status and Progress in the Diagnostic Approach" in *Current Urology 13* (4), January 2020. https://www.ncbi.nlm.nih.gov/pmc/articles/PMC6976999/

female, though they could impact that person's ability to have children. But some conditions are more complex.

For example, some children are conceived with male chromosomes (XY), but their developing bodies in the womb can't properly process the testosterone they produce—sort of like a radio exposed to a signal but unable to tune in. In this case, what often happens is that because the body doesn't get the signal to form male genitalia, it will form a vagina and labia instead. But the person doesn't have ovaries; instead, they have male gonads that don't descend. So, this person is chromosomally male, but their body ends up looking either female or sort of in-between.

Just this one example shows how complex disorders of sexual development can be! What, then, do we tell our kids? Little kids without a disorder of sexual development may not need to know about such complications yet, but we need to be sensitive to the fact that there may be kids in our churches in this situation and that our words may be hurtful to them or their parents if we talk as if there's never any question as to whether someone is male or female.

If your child has such a condition, or has a friend with that condition that the family is open about, then a conversation with your child will be necessary early on. It can be as simple as saying that God made our bodies good, but that because the world got troubled by Adam and Eve, all of our bodies face different troubles. These troubles don't mean that we're worse than anybody else. Jesus came to save us all. Even if our bodies have disorders now, we are all worthy of love and respect, and someday, when Jesus comes back, he will give all his people brand new bodies. What is more, no matter what our body is like now, we can praise him, serve him, and thank him.

For older kids who have some grasp of what transgender identities are, it can be helpful to talk about the difference between having a disorder of sexual development and adopting a transgender identity. When someone identifies as transgender, it's almost never because there is trouble with their physical body as such. They may experience gender dysphoria, which is real and painful, but this commonly exists with a body that is normally developed as male or female. A person with a disorder of sexual development, however, may need to figure out how to live in light of a body that sends multiple gender signals. Think about the person with XY chromosomes, for example, but who doesn't have typical male genitalia. As a disciple of Christ, that person will need to consider how to faithfully steward their body and should count on their Christian community to help them do that with grace and truth.

This is a brief introduction to a big topic, but for our kids the takeaways are still the good news that God created bodies good, and that no matter what difficulties we experience now, Jesus Christ helps us to honor him in these bodies as we await our new creation.

GAY RELATIONSHIPS AND SAME-SEX ATTRACTION

Just as God's vision for the goodness of male and female helps us with transgender identities and disorders of sexual development, so God's vision for marriage and singleness helps us navigate gay relationships and same-sex attraction.

Western culture, including the church in the West, has for many centuries been spinning a story that the most important relationship you can have in this world is a romantic one. At the same time, the other most powerful story being told in our society is that you need to look inside yourself in order to find out who you most truly are. To deny what you find in your heart will cause you to waste away and miss out on the best of life. One example that I was fed in my own childhood was Disney's *Beauty and the Beast*. Belle longs for "adventure in the great, wide somewhere" and intellectual stimulation, rather than marriage to Gaston. But she ends up with a handsome prince nonetheless.

When you combine these two stories of inner truth and necessary romance, as well as that of brokenness and sin, it is easy to see how so many people affirm gay relationships, even within the institutional Western church. If I look inside myself to find my true identity and I find attraction to other women, and if I've been told I have to be in a romantic relationship in order to be happy and full, the natural course of action seems to be to pursue a gay relationship. But these cultural stories only tell a partial truth: a partial truth that leads to death, not life.

We've already covered the half-truth of salvation-by-romance: God really did create us for a passionate, intoxicating, faithful love, and this great love, which

Jesus has for his people, is echoed in human longing for romantic love and in the one-flesh union of marriage. But other kinds of close relationship also echo God's great love for his people, including parent-child relationships, friendship, and siblinghood within the church. The lie is that romantic love is the *only* or *best* kind—the kind of love without which humans cannot flourish.

The other partial story—that our true selves are found inside ourselves and that we must obey whatever we find there—is just as troubling. The true part is that what we find inside of ourselves does tell us the truth. The piece that is obscured in the partial story is that what we find inside more often than not tells us bad news. Because of the Fall, our hearts are sick, sinful, small, petty, and mean. To only obey what I find in my heart is to become a slave to an unforgiving taskmaster. After all, the people most likely to just do all that they want are toddlers, and toddlers are not good models for how to live a responsible life. The message that we ought not be ruled by our feelings is good for all of us, including our kids. And it impacts how we think about same-sex attraction.

It is true that some of us experience, quite naturally it seems, romantic and sexual attractions to people of our same sex. This is true for me and true for many other disciples. To pretend this is *not* true, or to try to shove it away, doesn't help one bit. But it is equally damaging to throw up my hands and say, "Well, this is just how I feel, so I must do what I feel!" No. None of us have to be slaves to our natural feelings, because "natural" doesn't automatically mean good—or even neutral. Romantic and sexual desire for people of our same sex is a sinful result of the brokenness of the fall. And yet this brokenness and sin doesn't own us or define us. Christ has come to give us power by the Holy Spirit to live according to his "Yes," and God has given us by the Holy Spirit his perfect word, the Bible, which tells us what his "Yes" is. And the intended purpose of his design reveals why certain things won't work.

Think of it this way: when someone learns that a 20th-century car is designed to burn petrol for fuel, they can more easily grasp why putting milk or water into the tank will not only prevent the car from running but even damage its engine in the longer term. Similarly, when someone learns that marriage and singleness are first and foremost about telling the gospel, they'll have a better chance of seeing why God says that using sexuality in certain other ways ends up telling lies about the good news as well as damaging people. As we saw in chapter 1, one defining feature of marriage is meant to be faithfulness. So when people are unfaithful to their spouses, they tell a lie about how God relates to his people and how we should relate to them. Another defining feature of marriage is that it is the union of a man and a woman, because God intended a husband to represent God and a wife to represent God's people in displaying love across difference. When people enter into a union of a man and a man, or a union of a woman and a woman, they scramble the picture, telling lies about the gospel.

To summarize, this means our kids need at least three messages from us to prepare them to consider gay relationships and same-sex attraction wisely.

First, they need to know that our desires and feelings are not reliable; instead, we need the safe words of God, who has proven in Jesus that he loves us and is for us. We can talk about this in all areas so that it makes sense even before we get to sexuality.

When your child is caught in a lie, for example, you can talk about how covering up something bad we've done often *feels* like a safe choice because we're worried about punishment. But in reality, lies eventually always make things worse and hurt our relationships because they result in a lack of trust. Instead, your kids can always confess to you when they've done wrong because, even if there is a consequence, there will be forgiveness, just as God said.

Or when your child experiences anger and hits their sibling, you can explain (after the proper consequence and when everyone has calmed down) that we can get feelings inside that tell us that hurting someone will feel good or fix our problem—but this feeling lies to us. Hitting our sibling will not fix our problem. Instead, God says that when we feel angry, we need help to know what to do next. Our feelings matter a lot, but they always need to be tested against God's good wisdom.

Second, we need to repeat in various ways that although marriage is good, romance is not the definition of the good life; life with God and God's people is where satisfaction is found, no matter what our romantic relationship status is. This is just what we talked about at the end of chapter 1: spending time with church family and talking carefully about marriage and singleness really impacts our children.

Third, again as we discussed in chapter 1, we need to talk about the positive design of marriage frequently, so that when we encounter false visions, we have the right thing to compare them to. This just highlights how important the positive vision is for our children and how much we need it when we talk with them about LGBT+ questions.

Equipped with God's positive vision, with vocabulary around the biology of sexuality, and with an understanding of how brokenness and sin show up in bodies and relationships, we can now turn to some categories to use in talking to our kids directly about LGBT+ questions.

KEY PRINCIPLES

▲ Every human, every creature, and all of creation, has been impacted by sin and the fall. It is not one special category of people that are impacted—it is every single one of us.

◡ Christians are not surprised by the impact of Adam's and Eve's sin on bodies and relationships. We expect to see the effects of the fall in us and around us.

● Because of the fall and sin, Christians know that not every experience and feeling should be affirmed or followed.

PRACTICES FOR PARENTING

▪ Teach your children often about fallenness in the world:

- ⏤ If you know of a child born with a disability, you can teach your children that this doesn't mean that the child's disability was caused by a sin of theirs or their parent.

- ⏤ Instead, the sin of our first parents also caused corruption and brokenness to enter the world, impacting all of us.

- ⏤ Talk about events on the news, like destructive hurricanes or earthquakes, and help your children understand that creation itself is groaning and broken (Romans 8:22).

- ⏤ Jesus promises to come again someday to bring a new heavens and a new earth, and all who trust in him will receive new spiritual bodies that are no longer subject to corruption.

▲ Teach your children about the sinfulness of their own heart, as well as the heart of others.

- ⏤ Be willing to identify in your own life when you have a feeling that you shouldn't have acted on: "I'm sorry that I yelled at you. I was angry, and it wasn't okay that I treated you that way in my anger. Will you forgive me?"

- ⏤ This helps teach your child that all of us have to learn how to bring our feelings in line with God's will.

- This will prepare them for understanding why some people embrace LGBT+ identities and also help them not to think of these folks as radically different from us; instead, all of us need God's direction, power, and salvation!

4
TOOLS FOR LGBT+ CONVERSATIONS

"IT MAKES ME SO angry that people have turned something that is meant to be a sign of God's faithfulness into a symbol of something that is against God's word!"

A friend of mine was homeschooling her elementary-age kids when her eight-year-old made this comment about all the rainbow flags in their neighborhood. My friend's reaction struck me as precisely the right one. She admitted to her daughter that anger is often her first reaction too. She wanted her daughter to know that this is normal—but also to see that our anger can be an important gut check for us. Then she said, "Instead of being angry, let's decide that every time we see a rainbow flag, we're going to take a minute to pray for the people who put the flag up, that they would have a chance to hear the gospel and put their trust in Jesus." By saying this, my friend communicated to her children that the people who put rainbow flags up were people Jesus wanted them to love and pray for, rather than to judge or fear. The flags became a starting point for a gospel-centered conversation.

Of course, if you have younger kids, they may not even be aware of what the flags mean yet. My daughter has always been a fan of bright colors. The numerous displays of rainbow flags in our "progressive" city were, to her toddler self, not a political or cultural statement, but simply a pleasant feature of the neighborhood.

I'm sure many of you are in a position similar to my family's. The symbols of a movement are around your kids much earlier than they can understand the complex ideas that those symbols represent. Even more, we're regularly in contact with folks who identify as LGBT+. Not just random people but my daughter's teacher, her town soccer coach, and her local-branch librarian. These are kind, talented adults tasked in various ways with caring for and leading my daughter. At home and in church, she hears about the God who made and redeemed us, and who has a plan for our bodies and our relationships. Out in the world, she sees plenty of people she likes and admires who either seem to not know about this God and his plan or just don't care.

It's this difference between the message of home and church and the message of the world that most acutely raises the questions of this book for many of us. We can give our kids a lovely theological picture of bodies, singleness, and marriage. We can confidently and calmly explain where babies come from and how brokenness and sin impact everything. But where the rubber meets the road for many of us is when our four-year-old asks in the car ride, "Mom, can two daddies get married?"

In this chapter, we're going to consider how to shepherd our kids through these kinds of questions with Jesus' truth and grace. We'll start with some thoughts for our littlest kids and end with more complex ideas for older children.

KINGSHIP AND THE HOLY SPIRIT

When our kids are very young, they may not need to hear anything directly about gay relationships or people who identify as transgender. There is a type of oblivious innocence they can have, as with my daughter and the rainbow flags, that buys us some time. And what should we do with that time? Invest in teaching our kids the material in chapter 1 and chapter 2! That way, when they do eventually notice a gay relationship on a TV show (which is increasingly happening, as in the Netflix reboot of the superhero She-Ra) or in real life, we have a baseline to compare and contrast it to. This is why the positive vision is so crucial.

How then do we do this comparison when it does come up for our younger kids? There are sure to be ways that you and your church community could dream up together that would work well. But one tactic I used with my daughter was to talk in terms of the categories of kingship and the Holy Spirit.

Throughout her early life, as we talked about the gospel here and there, I would remind her that Jesus came to be many things to us, including our friend, our big brother, our Savior, and our King. In our household, her mom and dad have said "Yes" to Jesus, which means we say "Yes" every day to him as our good, wise, and trustworthy King. And we urge her, too, to say "Yes" to him because only he can love us perfectly, forgive our sins, and transform us from the inside out.

I found my daughter, like other little kids, really wanted to divide the world into good people and bad people. She sometimes would make statements to the effect that people who went to church must be good people and wondered if people who didn't go to church were bad people. We would assure her that according to God's word we're all born sinners and rebels, which means we're all born bad people. And that God's word also affirms that God himself created us, and died and rose again to save us! Which means we are all very loved and able to be rescued. The question to ask about each person is not "Is this a good person or a bad person?" but "Have they heard about the good King and Savior, Jesus?" And "Have they said, 'Yes' or 'No' to his offer of rescue and kingship?"

By offering her this category of kingship, we were giving her a way to understand why some people followed Jesus and obeyed him, and others did not. If we say "Yes" to Jesus, then we say "Yes" to his plans for our bodies, for our money, for our time, for everything. But if someone has not said "Yes" to Jesus, it makes sense that they won't obey his plans for their bodies, their money, or their time. This is not a safe place for anyone to be because only in

Jesus are we saved from our sin and the judgment that God will bring. But it does help us recognize why there are people—even nice, friendly people—who live so differently than Christians try to live.

So, with a show like *She-Ra*, if I choose to watch it with my child and she wants to understand why there are same-sex romantic relationships in that world, we could observe that God doesn't exist in that fictional world, so lots of things are different. And what is more, the people who made the show probably don't follow Jesus, so it makes sense that they will create characters who don't act in the way Jesus says is best.

When it came to her kindergarten teacher, I expressed to my daughter that I didn't think her teacher followed Jesus and so it wasn't a surprise if important parts of her life didn't match his commands. Or if your child asks you, "Can two daddies get married?" you could reply with something like "Jesus tells his people that marriage is only for a man and woman, which means it's not right for his followers to try to make marriage something else." If your child is ready for a bit more or is a bit older, you could observe with them that not all of your country's laws match God's laws, and that no one in your country is forced to follow Jesus, so sometimes it is legal to do something, even if God's people shouldn't do it. This can be tricky, but you'd be surprised how much your kids can understand. Following Jesus or not makes a real difference in how we live, and it's helpful for our children to see various ways in which this plays out.

It's not only with regards to sexuality, of course. We may need to repent when the ways in which we spend our money or time look more like the ways of the world than Jesus' vision for how we use money and time. But we of all people know that confession and repentance aren't death but life. And this brings up the other category we can use with our little kids: the Holy Spirit. The Bible teaches us that it is only by the power of God the Holy Spirit that we are born again, united to Christ, and enabled from the inside out to truly obey God from our hearts.

Even when we have Jesus as our King, we still struggle with feelings and desires that are not according to his plan. But he gives us his Holy Spirit so that we can have the power to repent and to grow in our obedience. The Christian life is learning how to rely not on ourselves but on the Spirit—a beautiful theme too big and rich to detail in this small book but essential to share with our kids, both in general and for LGBT+ questions. Why? Because along with kingship, it helps us see that we're not in and of ourselves different from people who don't follow Jesus. We're all born rebels with desires and temptations that are sinful and fallen. The difference for Christians is that we have a new King and a new power: the Holy Spirit. Someone who doesn't have Jesus as King won't have a reason to follow him nor the ability to do so from the heart. Encouraging our kids to see others in this way means we don't shame people, but we do recognize their great need because it's a need we share: to be saved from our sin.

AUTHENTICITY AND JUSTICE

I think the categories of Jesus' kingship and the Holy Spirit's help give our young kids so much. Yet as they get older, they may have more questions about *why* people support things like gay marriage and transgender identities. This is where the categories of authenticity and justice can be extremely helpful. Let me explain in a grown-up way, before we think about how to pass these ideas on to our kids.

The fact is that we humans don't support what we support simply because of solid rational arguments. No. Humans aren't just thinkers; we're also feelers. In fact, most often when we believe in something, it's because first we loved it, and then we saw that the reasons for it were good... or maybe we believed in dubious reasoning because we wanted whatever this was to be true.

The vast majority of people who support things like gay marriage and transgender identities aren't political activists. Nor are they people who consciously hate God and want to work against his rule. No, most people who support LGBT+ inclusion are just normal people. Most humans aren't trying to change the course of the world. We simply try to pay our bills, raise our kids, and watch our Netflix shows at night when we're tired. Our neighbors who support "progressive" sexual ethics are like this too— just trying to make a life. And for many of them, LGBT+ affirmation seems good, true, and beautiful because they value the concepts of justice and authenticity.

But authenticity and justice weren't invented by secularists; they exist in the West precisely because of the gospel. Although we Westerners live in post-Christian cultures today, the church has had a deeply influential impact on our past. So God is the one who taught us that we should love these concepts, even though they're often wielded today to fight for things that God's word condemns.

Take authenticity: the idea that we need to be our true selves, to look inside and discover who we are, and that to live differently than we feel is to live a lie. This idea didn't come from nowhere. It was Jesus who insisted that our inside life had to match our outside life (Matthew 23:27). It was God who declared that our hearts need to be right, flowing into right action (Isaiah 29:13). It was the church that built up a tradition of looking inward, so that we could look upward to God. Authenticity properly belongs to Christians.

And what about justice? The idea that wrongs should be righted and that humans deserve dignity, protection, and respect? This too belongs first and foremost to God. The Bible frequently demands that the poor, the migrant, the widow, and the orphan are defended and provided for (for example, Exodus 22:21-27). God is the one who declares bribes and oppression to be evil (Exodus 23:8). He is the one who will come to judge the living and the dead (1 Peter 4:5) and who guarantees that evil will not win in the end. Justice properly belongs to Christians.

For over a thousand years, the West was bathed in the goodness of these Christian concepts. But, over the last few centuries, for a variety of reasons, secularism has appeared in the West—a distortion of the gospel, like the reflection in a fun-house mirror. People and society wanted God's stuff but didn't want God. The West became like a rebellious teenager who claims to hate her parents but still wants to use their car. The on-the-ground effect we live with today is that our non-Christian neighbors often have certain Christian values but don't even recognize that they come from the gospel!

What is more, an appreciation of authenticity and justice (but without reference to God) are huge reasons why, for plenty of people, affirmation of LGBT+ identities and policies seems to make good sense.

As regards authenticity, most people in gay relationships are simply following their feelings, and many people who identify as transgender are also responding to something they perceive inside themselves. If we value obeying our inner selves, and cut out the God who warns us that our hearts are deceptive and infected with sin, then it makes a lot of sense to move towards LGBT+ affirmation.

As regards justice, many have either experienced, seen, or heard about ways in which people who identify as LGBT+ have been treated poorly, both in society in general and, tragically, by people who identify as Christians. This poor treatment has included things like physical abuse and even murder, as well as things like losing housing or employment simply on the basis of identifying as gay or transgender. If we value the respect, dignity, and fair treatment of all, then of course we will demand that mistreatment end and that any who perpetrated it be held accountable. This is something every Christian should eagerly affirm. Yet we disagree that historic and present mistreatment of those who identify as LGBT+ is a reason to abandon what God says about bodies and relationships. Instead, God's full vision must be obeyed: respect for all people, no matter what they believe, and insistence that his design for bodies and relationships is part of his holy word.

In this brief sketch, we can see how support of LGBT+ affirmation is complex; it overlaps with and even relies on Christian values in some places, and yet it stands in rebellion against God. This framework helps us to navigate LGBT+ questions because it helps us to think of ourselves primarily not as adversaries but as missionaries. And we can give our older kids a framework to think this way too, which I call Yes-No-Yes.

YES-NO-YES

This framework is a tool for helping us think in Christian ways about ideas, and it goes through three movements in this order: Yes-No-Yes. It is useful far beyond LGBT+ questions but is very helpful with them. Though it could seem complex at first, at its core it's a basic flow that even an eight-year-old could follow and that a teen or adult could use with sophistication.

The first Yes is listening to an idea, a story, or a person, and asking: what is being expressed that can be affirmed? Is this idea expressing a proper fear, which the Bible affirms we should be afraid of? Or perhaps a proper desire, which the Bible says is a good thing to desire? We should look for these points of connection knowing that because every person is created by God, we all still reflect him in certain ways, despite our sin.

As an example with LGBT+ questions, we've already seen a Yes to the idea of justice: that all people be treated with dignity and be safe from harm. As our kids encounter stories that include a call for justice for LGBT+ people, we can affirm that God demands this too, and that it is right to seek it.

The No movement is looking for how the idea, story, or person is in need of correction based on God's word. Perhaps we affirm a desire, but the way that desire is being pursued is destructive. Or perhaps we are able to validate a fear, and yet the way that fear is being alleviated goes against what God has said is good or right.

When it comes to justice in LGBT+ questions, some people have taken the valid call for an end to injustice and gone one step further: they now consider that the embrace and celebration of gay relationships is required for justice. To this, God's word says "No." If we don't look to the Bible for definitions of justice—which sometimes includes ideas that offend us or that make us uncomfortable—then eventually all of our practices of "justice" will become personal moves of preference and power. We will encourage sin, which is always wrong, and end up perpetrating trouble when what we wanted was a solution. These ideas are not too complex for a 10-year-old and can help them see that when left to our own devices, we make a mess, even if we have good intentions.

So what is the final Yes? It is a recognition of how God the Father's provision in Jesus Christ, applied by the Holy Spirit, is the only answer to our questions and troubles, chiefly of sin but of everything else as well. Because of Jesus' death, acts of injustice can be forgiven. Because of the Holy Spirit, communities and individuals can confront and change patterns of mistreatment or attitudes of disrespect. Folks who have received mistreatment can find healing and true paths of life, through the grace and truth of Christ. In fact, the resources of the gospel are boundless. Showing our children and dreaming with them about how Christ restores all things can help us become the people we are called to be in this generation.

Yes-No-Yes isn't a script; it's a way of being disciples in the world—of being salt and light. You'll notice it in the last chapter, for example, as the structure of the section on transgender identities. If your child wants to understand how to be a Christian in the world, this framework can be immensely helpful. Or perhaps your child isn't sure how they feel about faith in Jesus or Christianity; this framework can also help them see the way the gospel interacts with the world and how it offers the only and best way to true life.

MISSION

Yes-No-Yes teaches us to look for gospel bridges but also to be prepared to call out idols. As such, it is a great way to train ourselves and our children in the posture of mission: God first sent Jesus into the world and now is sending us, by the power of the Holy Spirit, to make disciples. Jesus came with both grace and truth (John 1:14)—and his mission requires both from us too.

Here, though, we might run up against a problem: often, we're either more of a grace person or more of a truth person. We find it hard to be both. If you're not sure which you tend to be, just ask a good friend. As for your child, you probably have a sense of which way they lean.

Both leanings present challenges and opportunities when it comes to mission related to LGBT+ questions. The grace person will naturally show deep love and compassion for LGBT+ neighbors, looking for ways to address wrongs and invite inclusion. The challenge is that this person will often shrink back from speaking painful truth, for fear of hurting people or losing the relationship. But there is also a beautiful opportunity: because the grace person so naturally loves that when they do take the risk of speaking truth, it can have a powerful impact because the person receiving that truth will be sure that they are for them.

The truth person will naturally show deep reverence and zeal for God's word and be eager to explain how his vision for our bodies and relationships isn't repressive but good. The challenge is that this person may have difficulty drawing near in loving ways to people who identify as LGBT+, for fear of signaling an affirmation of LGBT+ identities or of compromising with the world. But there is also a beautiful opportunity: because the truth person is so naturally zealous for God's word that when they do take the risk of showing love, it can have a powerful impact because the person receiving that love may recognize that this is a costly love reaching out across the divides.

Grace-leaning parents or grace-leaning kids who want to follow Jesus may need to remember that God's word is clear about sexual sin and about male and female, and it is never safe, wise, or loving to compromise on what God has declared. Sin is deceitful, and Jesus commanded that we remove the speck from our brother's eye (Matthew 7:3-5). There can be a tendency sometimes among those who are grace-leaning to think, "Ah well, no one is getting hurt, so what's really wrong?" This is a deadly way of thinking, and it gets the gospel wrong. Instead, the Holy Spirit through Paul commands us, "Take no part in the unfruitful works of darkness, but instead expose them" (Ephesians 4:11).

Truth-leaning parents or truth-leaning kids who want to follow Jesus may need to remember that God's word tells us that our enemy is not flesh and blood but the spiritual forces of evil in the heavenly places (Ephesians 6:12). Even when people are fully affirming of LGBT+ identities and advocating for changes in laws or schools, they are trapped by an ideology that doesn't love them— an ideology that is using them and that Jesus wants them to be saved from. Paul, who wrote those words to the Ephesians, faced a lot of human enemies, and yet he knew the truth: that every person is firstly a candidate for hearing the gospel and repenting. There can be a tendency sometimes among truth-leaning people either to isolate themselves away from the world to stay pure or to go on the attack. But neither is the way of Jesus, who went into the world to love people and to call them to repentance, and was willing to die to save the world.

There is a lot to consider as we think about mission in an age of LGBT+ affirmation. And we have to recognize that this aspect of the conversation is only appropriate for our children if they have said that they want Jesus as their King. If they haven't, then our primary task is to pray for them and continue to hold out the gospel to them. If they have, they're ready to consider mission. But that also means they need to consider the opposition they may face, which we turn to next.

KEY PRINCIPLES

▲ Your children need a way to help them understand why the rules and priorities of your family are different than other families, without casting shame on other people.

⌣ Our posture should be one of mission. By using principles like kingship and the Holy Spirit, Yes-No-Yes, and understanding why people are drawn towards things that God says no to, we can help our children think about how to engage with their non-Christian neighbors with grace and truth, rather than fear and exclusion.

PRACTICES FOR PARENTING

● Use the concepts of kingship and the Holy Spirit with your kids:

    — Talk about how having Jesus as our King means we need to pay close attention to him and his words so we know what is good and what is bad.

— Remind your kids (and yourself) that we can't obey our King without being empowered by the Spirit. Model prayers like "Holy Spirit, please help us see today where we are not obeying you, and give us the ability to confess our sin and practice good."

— Teach your children that not all people have Jesus as their King, and that everyone deserves a chance to hear about his kingdom and enter in. Help them to see that only people who follow King Jesus will be able to follow his rules from the heart.

■ For older kids who are especially interested in understanding LGBT+ questions, have them read through the section on authenticity and justice. Ask them what questions they still have and what it might mean to relate well to people who identity as LGBT+.

▲ Practice Yes-No-Yes as your family engages in normal life: watching movies, listening to songs, or noticing what festivals your community puts on.

— Ask often, "What part of this is something God would say 'Yes' to? How do we know?" This teaches your children to always go back to the Bible.

— Ask often, "What part of this is something God would say no to? How do we know?"

— I have one friend who with every commercial, for example, would ask his children, "What are they trying to sell you, and how?" which is another way of getting to the same destination.

— Ask often, "How could Jesus' saving or healing make a difference here?" The ability of our older kids to think of ways that might happen could surprise us.

5

FEAR NOT

"**I DON'T MEAN TO BE** dramatic, but I think I may be going through something a little bit like what Jesus is talking about here." My friend's oldest daughter was pointing to Jesus' words in Luke 6:22-23: "Blessed are you when people hate you and when they exclude you and revile you and spurn your name as evil, on account of the Son of Man! Rejoice in that day, and leap for joy, for behold, your reward is great in heaven; for so their fathers did to the prophets."

This young woman attends a very "progressive" middle school here in Massachusetts. She is a gentle, thoughtful follower of Jesus, without a cruel bone in her body. And yet, at the age of eleven, she was cut off by some of her closest friends when they realized she wasn't toeing the party line on LGBT+ celebration—cut off simply for her charitably held beliefs, not for any acts of oppression or unkindness. Many of our Christian siblings around the world suffer much more for their profession of faith than social rejection; nonetheless, my young friend experienced a real and painful cost for her faithfulness to Christ at school. And it is this kind of cost, as well as sharper ones, that we are beginning to fear for our children.

When we encounter situations like this, we find ourselves crying, "It's simply not *fair!*" We can feel that in our bones. Yet how are we to respond, and how are we to teach our children who follow Jesus to respond?

As parents and teachers, we know we need to help our kids respond to unfair situations with grace, and this often requires helping them discern what is worth protesting and what should simply be accepted. When dealing with sibling squabbles, some of us have repeated, "You get what you get, and you don't get upset" so many times that it feels like a memory verse (2 Parenting 10:21). But of course, we never deny the fundamental importance of justice itself, nor the idea of fairness. We know that "the LORD sits enthroned forever; he has established his throne for justice" (Psalm 9:7), and we too are to become people of justice. We know that justice is good, and we want our children to grow into adults who value and practice it.

Our sense of justice gets piqued when we see any person getting punishment or consequences that they don't deserve, like my friend's daughter at middle school. More and more, Christian ethics are no longer seen as respectable, nor even merely quaint or slightly behind the times. No, there is a rising sense that Christian sexuality is oppressive and harmful, and that those who hold these views are bigots. It's not an irrational fear that if we train our children to value God's vision for bodies and relationships—and if they decide they want to really follow Jesus—they may be judged for this, even if they hold their views with kindness.

A RETURN TO THE NEW TESTAMENT

In the West today, it seems that we are returning—slowly and unevenly but surely—to the normal conditions of discipleship that the New Testament describes: a situation in which claiming the name of Christ involves real social cost, often painful. If our children choose to be disciples, then they will face this cost at a younger and more tender age than most of us had to. In the West, Christianity experienced long centuries of dignity, especially where I live in the United States. Perhaps when we were younger, being a Christian was something respected—something which received a positive reaction from the people of this world. But this is actually different from what the New Testament declares will be the normal experience of the Christian in a non-Christian world. And it's changed.

It isn't our fault that we grew up in unusual times. But because our children are facing different conditions, we can feel remarkably unequipped. The kindness of our God, however, is that he has not left us on our own, lost and without help. We have in our Scriptures exactly what we and our children need to face these new circumstances.

Jesus in fact told us what we can expect in his farewell speech to his disciples before he went to the cross: "If the world hates you, know that it has hated me before it hated you. If you were of the world, the world would love you as its own; but because you are not of the world, but I chose you out of the world, therefore the world hates you. Remember the word that I said to you: 'A servant is not greater than his master.' If they persecuted me, they will also persecute you" (John 15:18-20).

On some level, we wish for verses where Jesus would say that he took all of the hard things for us, and that our lives and the lives of our children will only go from strength to strength, path cleared. Mercifully, Jesus did take the hardest thing of all: by dying on the cross in our place, he absorbed the condemnation we deserved and gives us in exchange his righteous standing before God, as well as the Holy Spirit to empower us. But God has not yet brought the new heavens and the new earth; we remain here, in a land of danger and temptation. And it's precisely because of this danger and temptation that Jesus gives us warnings.

No parent would send their child on a journey without warning them of what they might face. My daughter is old enough now to walk home from school on her own, but she is warned to only cross the main street at the light, where she is more protected from the cars that speed along. I give her this warning and command precisely because I love her. Similarly, Jesus warns his disciples because he loves them, and his warning is that they will be treated just as he was.

And how, precisely, was Jesus treated? He moved through his earthly ministry with perfect love in his every motivation and action—and was brutally murdered on false charges nonetheless. Sometimes we can hope, without even expressing it, that if the motivations and actions of ourselves and our children are sufficiently Christian, then our sincerity and love will be recognized, and we'll be protected from misunderstanding and mistreatment.

That can happen, by God's good grace. But it is never promised. Nor is it what Jesus tells us to prepare for. Among other things, he plainly warned his first disciples that they would be hated by the world if they follow him, because the world hated him first. If our children want to follow Jesus, then we must expose them to this warning, which was given in love.

Yet this is not the only word. Jesus was stark about the reality of mistreatment because he did not want his disciples to be caught unaware, thinking they'd been abandoned by God. But he was just as firm in his promises of blessing in the midst of mistreatment: "Blessed are those who are persecuted for righteousness' sake, for theirs is the kingdom of heaven. Blessed are you when others revile you and persecute you and utter all kinds of evil against you falsely on my account. Rejoice and be glad, for your reward is great in heaven, for so they persecuted the prophets who were before you" (Matthew 5:10-11).

It takes faith to believe what Jesus is saying in this passage because, normally, being reviled, persecuted, and gossiped about looks and feels like the opposite of blessing. The blessing he is promising is, in a way, hidden. The mistreatment, though, is obvious.

Jesus is talking about mistreatment that comes in two ways: (1) falsely and (2) on his account. This text isn't meant to cover over when our kids are sinning and suffer the just consequences. This text is talking about the reality that following Jesus means being falsely accused, just as he was. But even more, God is the one who sees it—and the one who blesses that follower and rewards them. Just as the mistreatment wasn't fair, so the blessing isn't either; it's beautifully more than fair—it is grace for disciples earned by Christ.

This, then, is what we need to give our children to equip them for this moment: the exact warnings and the exact promises that Christ himself gave us in his word.

RECORD SCRATCH: FEARS THAT FOLLOW GOD'S PROMISES

As we encounter these warnings and promises, several things may be happening in our own hearts.

First, we're confronted with a haunting question: Do I really believe this? Do I believe that God's blessing and reward is more satisfying than the love and approval of the world? It is possible that these questions and situations facing your children are pressing on doubts and insecurities in your own faith in Christ and that part of your fear about equipping your children is that you are trying to give them what you yourself do not fully possess.

If this is you, do not lose heart. Remember that God's face towards you in Christ is one of love. He is always saying, *Return to me because of my great love for you.* The gospel is the good news of forgiveness and life, which we don't deserve, earned for us by Jesus' death and resurrection. Sin and doubt grow in the dark, like a fungus. Tell someone who loves Jesus and loves you of your fears and doubts; take up the word and prayer. God promises to meet and restore you as you seek him.

Second, Jesus' warnings and promises confront us with another frightening possibility. We may fully believe the warnings and promises Christ makes about discipleship. We may feel ready to teach these to our children. But perhaps we fear that our children, looking at the cost, will consider it too high and walk away from Jesus.

If we're honest, this is perhaps the greater fear prompted by our changing culture: not merely that our children could be mistreated for their faith but that they won't find Jesus more worthy of their allegiance than the world and that the social inconvenience of being a Christian will prove so difficult for them that they drop Jesus altogether. Or perhaps they will be convinced by the world's sexual ethic and find it more beautiful than God's.

I say this because I feel this fear myself, as a parent and as a campus minister who has seen many college students walk away from the faith their parents hold. Responding to *this* fear could merit an entire book. In the meantime, here is where I am taking shelter: God in Christ loves our children even more than we do.

This isn't the same as a promise that each and every one of them will be saved. The mystery of God's love is that he gives us the freedom to accept or reject it. This must drive us to prayer and to seeking the help and advice of our Christian community. Our role as parents is to proclaim the whole true gospel, by the power of the Holy Spirit, and trust God with the rest. Not to judge ourselves, and certainly not to judge others, based on whether our kids follow Christ or not. Instead we are invited to trust him—to choose to believe that he is good. Now is the time to press into deeper faith and trust, not fearing the hard questions but seeking in them a road to greater intimacy with our Creator and Savior. As we wait on him, we equip our children as best we can.

THE WARNINGS AND PROMISE LIVED OUT

Once you start looking in the Bible for this reality of a discipleship that is costly but rewarding, you will find it all over the place. One helpful place in which to look is in the Old Testament book of Daniel.

The stories told in Daniel come at a painful time in the history of God's people, the Israelites. Throughout many generations, the land they lived in had been an important symbol of their relationship with God. This was especially true of the city of Jerusalem, where the temple was built by King Solomon. But God had warned them for centuries, through various prophets, that if they continued to practice injustice and sin, he would banish them from that land as a punishment. He gave them so much time to repent, but they hardened their hearts. Finally, and horrifically, God sent foreign nations to conquer the land and drag the Israelites away. This is known as the Exile.

The book of Daniel follows some of these Israelites who were taken captive to Babylon as young men— probably when still teenagers. This land was totally unlike Jerusalem; instead of being surrounded by symbols of the true God, they were surrounded by idols. Even more, they were taken into service at the Babylonian court, given new Babylonian names, and taught the language, culture, and religion of Babylon. Everything around them was designed to turn them into Babylonians, pressuring them to leave the God of their ancestors behind.

In certain ways, our children's story will be similar. I'm not trying to suggest that in the West today we've experienced a trauma like that of the fall of Jerusalem or forced removal from our homes. Nonetheless, as our children grow up with fewer and fewer people attending churches and professing faith, more of them will be like these Israelite youths. The secular West has its own myths, language, and literature. It has its own idols, its own demands for what people worship (whether self, progress, or whatever), and its own tactics for trying to force people to toe the line. All this and more is communicated through our movies, songs, advertisements, and social media. Secular culture exerts an incredible amount of pressure on adults and is incredibly formative for children. And especially in areas with fewer committed Christians, it can feel as if our children stand no chance. As I scan the parents in my local church, I realize that it is not uncommon for their children to be the only kid in their grade at school with believing parents—one of the only kids with church as a regular and meaningful part of life. It's true at this point for my own child. Perhaps it's true of your child too.

The experiences of Daniel and his three friends, Shadrach, Meshach, and Abednego, show us what it can look like to cling to the Lord in a culture flowing in the other direction. More than that, it can show us what God's care in the midst of such a culture can look like too. Our God is the same today as he was in those centuries ago; both we and our children can take comfort in how he is able to provide.

The Israelite youths at times faced sophisticated opposition. At one point, King Nebuchadnezzar erects a golden image and demands that everybody worship it. Soon enough, "certain Chaldeans came forward and maliciously accused the Jews" (Daniel 3:8). Knowing that Shadrach, Meshach, and Abednego would never worship this image, these certain Chaldeans (another term for Babylonians) present this to the king as a political threat, and he responds by enforcing capital punishment. This reminds us that the worship of idols always produces resistance and violence against those who refuse to bow.

We saw in the last chapter that many people deeply believe in LGBT+ affirmation because they find it good, true, and beautiful. On a societal level, there is also a strong movement of political and cultural activists who demand that all people embrace LGBT+ affirmation in the ways that they themselves do. This movement is, in its own way, a kind of religion; it evangelizes, it seeks to bring others into alignment with its moral code, and it tries to punish those who are out of line. When anyone, including Christians, falls short of full LGBT+ affirmation, there are consequences. It is not unlike being an exiled Israelite refusing to bow to Chaldean idols.

But note, too, what Daniel 3 also says: it was not all the Chaldeans who used this tactic against the youths but only "certain" of them. Similarly, today it is not *all* supporters of the LGBT+ movement who aggressively oppose others. We can teach our children to expect that some organized opposition to God's people will come, while also protecting them from the simplistic view that all who reject the Lord are actively out to attack us.

This nuanced reality can be seen in a later story, this time during the reign of King Darius. A group of officials maliciously accused Daniel of subverting Darius' rule by his refusal to stop praying to the Lord (Daniel 6:7, 12-13). The prescribed punishment was death—by being thrown into a den of lions. But interestingly, this time, we see that Darius himself, a pagan, was distressed by this threat to Daniel's life (v 14)—so distressed that he "spent the night fasting" (v 18). There was something about Daniel's integrity which meant that although Daniel refused to follow Darius' gods, Darius still desired good for Daniel. In this we hear an echo of Jesus' words: "Let your light shine before others, so that they may see your good works and give glory to your Father who is in heaven" (Matthew 5:16). Indeed, when, the next morning, Daniel was lifted from the den alive—having been miraculously saved by the Lord—Darius issued a decree that his subjects were to "tremble and fear before the God of Daniel, for he is the living God, enduring forever" (Daniel 6:26). As for Daniel, so for us: although some may be out to attack us, others will acknowledge the truth and goodness we live by.

So we can take courage from these Israelite exiles living among idolatry. We see that assimilation to idolatry is not automatic. The young men had every opportunity to believe and behave as Chaldeans—they were steeped in that culture while young. Yet God sustained them. He is powerful. He was able to shut the mouths of lions and keep the blazing furnace from even singeing the young men's clothing. He is also worthy: Daniel and his friends were ready to risk so much only because they knew that God deserved their worship and total allegiance. One of my favorite moments in the entire book is when Shadrach, Meshach, and Abednego tell Nebuchadnezzar that God is quite able to save them from the furnace but also that *even if God chooses not to save them*, they still will not bow down to the idol (Daniel 3:17-18). Their allegiance to the Lord is based on God's worthiness, not on what he will do for them. Targeted, unjust persecution did not break them. And it need not break our children either.

We can trust that God is able to give our children grace under pressure—and as we teach them these Bible stories, they can see that too. This confidence in God's power, his goodness, and his worthiness—confidence that, like that of Daniel's friends, endures *even if we are not spared*—is available to our children and to us today.

Centuries later, Jesus warned, "Do not fear those who kill the body but cannot kill the soul. Rather fear him who can destroy both soul and body in hell. Are not two sparrows sold for a penny? And not one of them will fall to the ground apart from your Father. But even the hairs of your head are all numbered. Fear not, therefore; you are of more value than many sparrows" (Matthew 10:28-31). We need to fear not men but God, and even this fear is actually a refuge in the Father's love. This is the refuge we need and that we need to offer to our children.

Though there is growing societal pressure to celebrate and embrace a vision of gender and sexuality that is at odds with God's good vision, we do not need to be ruled by fear. Yes, our children may face opposition that we might never have had to deal with at their age. Yes, there will be pressure to take the easy way out—to turn away from Jesus because of the cost. But this is also a beautiful time to be a disciple; when the contrast between God's ways and the world's ways is sharper, the glorious goodness of the gospel shines all the more brightly.

KEY PRINCIPLES FROM THIS CHAPTER

▲ The Bible warns that following God will bring real costs but also real rewards.

◡ God is able to keep his people faithful, even when they are surrounded by idolatry and persecution.

PRACTICES FOR PARENTING

● With younger children, teach the stories in Daniel. As they get to know the brave young men and their mighty God, they will be introduced to important themes that can be built on later.

  — You might do this during a bedtime routine or around the breakfast table, or set aside a family

Bible time on Sunday afternoon. Be creative and ask other friends at your church for ideas.

■ Older children might be ready to consider either (1) the deeper themes from the Daniel stories that are shared in this chapter or (2) a passage like Matthew 5:11-12.

– If your child likes to read and study, you could set up a special time to talk together about what they notice in these passages, how it makes them feel, and what these passages teach us about God. You don't need to know all the answers—just having the conversations can be a great way to engage with your kid!

– If your child doesn't enjoy much study, you could casually share with them what you have learned about either passage in the car, around the dinner table, or on a walk. They may seem as if they don't care to hear, but children are often listening more than we think they are, and seeing your reaction to the Bible will be deeply formative.

▲ If you feel insecure about your own ability to read or teach the Bible, you're not alone! There is always time to take a small step forward. Ask friends at church or in your small group for ideas and accountability in your own growth.

ᝰ If your kids at school identify as Christians and get some pushback for that, use some material from this chapter to help them see both Jesus' warnings and his promises.

- Help your children see that while some non-Christians may oppose them, many others will not. We don't want them to grow fearful but to have a humble confidence in Jesus.

6

IN THE FAMILY

"I RAISED MY DAUGHTER IN the church faithfully, but she went off to college, and now she's telling me she thinks God blesses gay marriage. What should I do?"

"I homeschooled my children and taught them God's truth. But my 18-year-old son just told me he's gay and doesn't consider himself a Christian anymore. I'm scared and heartbroken. What do I do?"

I have gotten scores of emails from parents telling stories just like these. They are desperate for help and often blindsided by what they are faced with. Up to this point, we've mostly been considering the way to disciple our kids when LGBT+ questions arise because of what is happening *out there*, in the world. But as we end, we need to consider various ways that the questions can arise *in here*: that is, both in the church and in our families. We will turn our attention, then, to two items: what if these questions are personal for my children, and how do we respond to professing Christians who celebrate full LGBT+ affirmation?

POTENTIAL CONFUSION FOR YOUNG CHILDREN

I've argued that we need to tell our children early and often about God's design for sexuality so that they can understand how the messages that society gives them are different. Yet, even if we provide good descriptions of the positive vision, little kids can still easily get confused, just based on the way society describes LGBT+ phenomena.

For example, your young daughter might hear from someone in the neighborhood that being gay is when a woman loves another woman, and how that's great because love is great. This could raise a number of questions for you daughter! She might wonder whether, since she feels real love for her friends who are girls, that means she's gay. It would be easy to see how she got here. This is where we can go back to God's positive vision: God affirms that all humans need love and that love is indeed great! But it is only great when lived out according to God's good rules. He says that the right way to love people of the same sex is in friendship—and especially the love relationship that exists between siblings in Christ. So, yes, your daughter should love her friends deeply! This doesn't mean she is gay; it means that she is human. We clarify what God says love is, over and over.

Or take another example. Maybe your young son hears at school that boys like rough-and-tumble play and girls like chatting and crafts. But perhaps your son is a sensitive boy who prefers calm and quiet to being tussled about. This could raise a question for him: does this mean he's really a girl? Or does this mean God got it wrong by making him a boy? You could see how, based on what he's hearing, he might think that. But this is where we go back to God's positive vision: no, God didn't make a mistake by making him a boy! Society makes a mistake when they say boys can't also love calm and quiet. There are lots of healthy ways to be a boy and lots of healthy ways to be a girl. Our bodies tell us the truth about whether we are male or female, and we are free to see what gifts and interests we have and enjoy them, in relationship with the Lord.

IF YOUR CHILD COMES OUT

But we also need to consider that, as our children grow older, some of them will discover that they do experience same-sex attraction or perhaps feelings of gender dysphoria. After all, we know that the Fall has impacted every human person, and its impact could include these experiences for some of the children we care about. So how should we prepare for this possibility, without panic?

It's important to note that children tend to notice feelings of same-sex attraction or gender dysphoria long before they tell anyone. This can be a lonely and terrifying experience. I've talked to many adult disciples who grew up going to church, who noticed these experiences in childhood or adolescence and went into complete denial or desperately tried to pray the feelings away for years, to no avail. They often worried that if they disclosed these experiences to their parents, they would be utterly rejected. They sometimes worried also whether these experiences meant that God would not accept them.

If you have spent their childhood speaking calmly and confidently about the bodies God gave us and how reproduction works, your children will be better able to trust that you know what you're talking about when it comes to sexuality. If you spend their childhood speaking of people who identify as LGBT+ in tones of respect—in ways that don't reduce them to their sexual choices and that don't identify them as enemies—your children will feel safer coming to you with their own feelings that may be big and scary.

If our children don't feel that we are safe enough to talk to, they will find someone who is... or who they mistakenly think is. They will ask their friends. They will ask the internet. They will ask in places where we can't be sure that the information they get will be true, good, or beautiful. While we cannot guarantee that our children will confide in us, if we speak early and often about sexuality in ways that are calm, confident, and respectful, we will greatly increase the odds that they will.

In our church, we have a number of adult disciples who (like me) came to Christ with a history of same-sex sexual relationships and a number who have been followers of Jesus since childhood and found themselves starting to experience same-sex attraction in adolescence. Because the kids in our church know some of these stories, they have a mental category for faithful followers of Jesus who experience same-sex attraction and do not pursue their feelings. They know that they won't be mocked, rejected, or treated like an emergency if they find themselves romantically drawn to their same sex but that their church family will treat this like any other area of temptation. If you don't have adults in your church who have been open about their own experiences of same-sex attraction, it's worth telling your kids about some of the Christians in public ministry who have written faithfully out of their own experience of same-sex attraction, so that children in your church have this category too.

The moment when a child discloses an experience like same-sex attraction or gender dysphoria is crucial. What they need most from you in that moment is to be reassured of your love for them. Thank them for sharing with you, give them a hug, tell them you love them, and just give them space. You can ask them how long they have noticed these feelings and how you can help.

They don't need a reiteration of what the Bible teaches right in that first conversation; if you have been teaching them along the way, they already know what the Bible teaches. What they need is to know that you see them, that you love them, and that you are there to help guide them. You won't know what specific help your child needs until you ask more, over the course of various conversations, about how you can come alongside them.

You, of course, will also be feeling all kinds of things if your child discloses this kind of experience to you. Maybe it takes you entirely by surprise; maybe you've been expecting it. Your emotions also matter, and it is important that you have a place in which to process those emotions away from your child, and in a way that keeps what they have shared with you as confidential as possible. This means getting support from one or two discreet, trusted people who love you and Jesus and your family. Your child's trust in you will be impacted by how you wield this sensitive information they have shared, so make sure it doesn't become an item of gossip.

There are so many reasons why a child may disclose something like this to you. With same-sex attraction, it could be tempting as a parent to dismiss this experience as something like a phase. I would urge you, however, not to be dismissive. If your child is young, early in puberty perhaps, there may be real confusion about how they feel—but if they're taking the scary step of telling you, it's probably not based on nothing. Listen with curiosity and care, and assure them that no matter what they feel, you're there to love and help them. Remind them that the earliest days of emerging adulthood are often the most confusing, but that there is no pressure to know perfectly what they feel. The world may put this pressure on them because society demands that a person build their core identity on sexuality. But in Christ, we know our core identity is in Jesus, and so everything else that is true about us (good, bad, or neutral) is submitted to him.

If your child is older when they disclose same-sex attraction to you—a teenager or in their twenties—it is likely that this experience has endured for some time. Again, thank them for sharing with you, don't panic, and ask them honoring questions. An honoring question is a question that doesn't shame or accuse but that honestly seeks understanding and connection. If your child has chosen to follow Jesus, then this experience of same-sex attraction need not derail or define them. Having these feelings doesn't mean that your child will pursue them. As a parent, you can be there to help them learn how to thrive in Christ no matter what temptations they face.

A disclosure of gender dysphoria, or a desire to adopt a trans identity, brings its own challenges. A small percentage of the population experiences gender dysphoria; while often these experiences resolve with puberty and adulthood, sometimes they do not. Children with these experiences need care, understanding, and discipleship. The world will be telling them that the only solution to these feelings is to adopt a trans identity. The gospel counters this, speaking instead of Jesus Christ, who came to vindicate creation and will one day give us new, spiritual bodies like his own. Can we become a patient community of grace and truth that trusts in and looks for this together with our children?

As we discussed earlier, some children may want to adopt a transgender identity for reasons apart from gender dysphoria. For example, there has been a growing trend of adolescent females who have never shown signs of gender confusion in childhood choosing to adopt a transgender identity as teens. While it's controversial to say so, there is a social aspect to the rapid increase of these identities among young adults. As parents, we are responsible for guiding our children; this includes speaking the truth about their sex and gender to them, with calm confidence. It may even include removing them from certain social contexts (in person and online) if the influences over them are proving confusing and destructive. A calm posture of watchful waiting with any child who is in this position is best.

This little volume can only barely touch on these realities. What I want to reiterate here, though, is that we can only gain by speaking early, often, and appropriately to our children about sexed bodies and the gift of sexuality stewarded as God calls us to. We don't know what they will face, but by the power of the Spirit we can seek to equip them for the journey.

What we don't have control of for our children is what journey they want to take: with and towards Jesus or without him and away from him? Or what if they want to walk with Jesus but want to do so in the midst of LGBT+ affirmation? We'll consider these possible outcomes now.

IF YOUR CHILD LEAVES THE FAITH

The wonderful news, as we discussed earlier, is that an experience of same-sex attraction or gender dysphoria does not define your child. Many children in this category will long to follow and obey Jesus, and so will seek to submit all of their experiences to him. Your role as a parent is to be a trusted, loving source of guidance in the Christian life. Even if you don't experience these same temptations, sharing wisdom from your own battles of saying "No" to the flesh and "Yes" to Jesus will enrich your children's faith. What is more, you may learn a lot yourself from watching your kids choose faithfulness in the midst of a generation that tells them they are foolish to deny their feelings for the sake of Christ.

At the same time, we recognize that despite our best efforts, we may have children who choose not to follow the Lord. We mentioned this fear in the last chapter and acknowledged that children may make this choice for all kinds of reasons, regardless of their position on LGBT+ questions. It's important that you not assume that, if your child does not want to walk with Jesus, it is because of their experience of same-sex attraction, for example. Perhaps it is, but perhaps they have other more primary objections. Keep dialogue open with your kids to understand their resistance or hesitation as they describe it.

If you have spent their childhood bringing them to church and teaching them the gospel, their rejection of Jesus may also feel like a rejection of you. There are so many feelings that can arise, each of which needs a safe place in which to be processed. Remember that salvation is always a free gift of grace and that God loves to work through the prayers of his people. While your children have breath, there is always hope that they will turn to Jesus.

I've talked with many parents of adult children who have walked away from the faith in order to embrace a transgender identity or a gay relationship. Not one of these parents has been able to tell me about this without tears. Every time, they ask some version of "What can I do? What should I do?" My advice is to pray for their child, to fast for them, and to radically love them. As parents, we know that love is never equal to full affirmation of choices—in a whole range of areas. But it is probable that your child is hearing from peers, or on the internet, or in the culture that if you don't affirm their LGBT+ identity, then you are a nasty, hateful bigot who does not love them. They may even want to cut you out of their life. It pains me to even type that, but I know it happens. In this case, remember that prayer is powerful. So pray without giving up. But if there is still a relationship held out, ask yourself, "In what ways can I show radical love to my child that might confound the messages they hear?" This will look different in every situation, but be assured that spending time with your child, offering to pray for them, and asking about their friends and lives is not the same thing as condoning any of the choices they make.

Your adult children will certainly be well aware of what you think about the gospel and sexuality, if you have taught them. What they might not be sure of is whether you love them. In fact, because our culture says you *cannot* love someone who identifies as LGBT+ without affirming their identity, they might be primed to doubt your love for them because you clearly don't affirm their choices.

Pray for wisdom, consult with your Christian community, and consider how to love your child well and whether there could be any opportunity for gospel conversation. I would prioritize talking about Jesus and his offer of salvation over conversations about sexuality for the child who has walked away from God because their primary need is reconciliation to the Lord. However, if they initiate conversations on sexuality and Christianity, by all means engage! We never know how the Spirit may be tugging on our children to bring them back to the gospel.

REVISIONIST CHRISTIANITY

But there is also a possibility that your child will try to have both: a relationship with Jesus *and* a committed gay relationship or a transgender identity. You may also have a child who does not identify as LGBT+ but still affirms these identities and wants to support them as a Christian. This is what's sometimes called a "revisionist" position (because it embraces a "revised" version of the church's historic teaching). In my mind, this is the toughest area of the conversation.

People usually want to try to have both of these things because they see the goodness of Jesus and have no conscious desire to walk away from him, yet there is also something about LGBT+ affirmation that strikes them as right or even godly. Perhaps they look at the historic mistreatment of people who identified as LGBT+ and, seeing that Jesus would never act like that, wonder if the church has got the whole thing wrong. Or they believe that romance is necessary for fulfillment (especially if they grew up in a church that only taught about marriage, not singleness) and so naturally think that their friends who identify as gay deserve that too. Of course, others who, for example, experience exclusive, powerful same-sex attraction may simply think, "Why would God allow me to feel such a strong desire for something that isn't hurting anyone, if it isn't okay?"

There are myriad reasons, and you won't know which appeal to your child unless you ask. And it's possible that you yourself lean towards this affirmation or aren't sure where you stand. In either or both cases, I strongly recommend checking out Rebecca McLaughlin's *Does the Bible Affirm Same-Sex Relationships?*—a short, easy-to-read book that works through ten of the most popular arguments that people make in favor of monogamous same-sex relationships for Christians and why none of them ultimately hold water. At the time of writing this, I don't know of a comparable volume engaging with affirming arguments for transgender identities, but Preston Sprinkle's *Embodied* is a thoughtful Christian treatment of the topic in general. Educating yourself on various ways in which people end up embracing revisionist positions will help as you listen to and engage with your children. This is true even if your children don't currently hold to a revisionist view, because these views are on the rise and are enticing.

If your child is professing faith in Jesus, then they are your brother or sister in Christ. And our responsibility to all our siblings in Jesus is to "exhort one another every day, as long as it is called 'today,' that none of you may be hardened by the deceitfulness of sin" (Hebrews 3:13). Sin is not a plaything; it is not safe. It must be confronted. But how?

For guidance, we have no better text than Matthew 7:1-5; it equally helps and confronts both those of us who are "grace people" and those of us who are "truth people," as we consider how to exhort our children who are in error on sexuality and the Bible. Jesus said:

Judge not, that you be not judged. For with the judgment you pronounce you will be judged, and with the measure you use it will be measured to you. Why do you see the speck that is in your brother's eye, but do not notice the log that is in your own eye? Or how can you say to your brother, 'Let me take the speck out of your eye,' when there is the log in your own eye? You hypocrite, first take the log out of your own eye, and then you will see clearly to take the speck out of your brother's eye. (Matthew 7:1-5)

The "grace person" is liable to hear Jesus say, "Judge not, that you be not judged" and think, "Well, maybe that means let things be. No one is perfect, and being judgmental is off-putting." The trouble is that these words come in the context of the Sermon on the Mount—a famous section of teaching where Jesus actually makes much of the Old Testament law tighter than it seemed to his audience. He taught that it was not only murder that deserved judgment but unrighteous anger and insults (5:21-22); and that it wasn't only adultery that was sin but also looking at a woman in lust (v 27-30).

This same sermon wouldn't then state that we shouldn't exhort each other to live and believe rightly. No! After Jesus says not to judge, he says, "First take the log out of your own eye, and then you will see clearly to take the speck out of your brother's eye" (7:5). Some of us may wish he'd said, *Take the log out of your eye, and then sit down and be quiet.* But no: he urges you to remove your brother's (or your child's) speck. If the thought of doing that makes you nervous, you're probably in a better place to do it, if you seek the power of the Spirit.

Those of us who are "truth people" may be very ready to remove our brother's speck. The word we need to pay careful attention to is "Why do you see the speck that is in your brother's eye, but do not notice the log that is in your own eye? ... You hypocrite, first take the log out of your own eye" (v 3, 5). God's word is very clear on his plan for our bodies and our relationships. Nonetheless, you must search your heart for your attitude in regard to exhorting your child or others. For instance, it's worth asking yourself if you would have the same level of concern if your child was engaging in sexual sin with someone of the opposite sex. Or would you be okay with that yet eager to confront them if they were being drawn into same-sex sexual sin? All too often, Christian parents have held to a double standard, whereas the New Testament takes all forms of sexual sin very seriously. There is likely some log that needs removing from your own eye; taking out specks can only happen truly in humility, by the power of the Spirit.

As long and as far as we are able to, we seek to urge our children to trust Jesus as Lord and Savior. If they profess to do so, then we seek to urge them to reject sin and embrace righteousness. Perhaps we may be able to convince them, by God's power—and perhaps we'll receive helpful correction ourselves along the way in how we hold our own views. And in all things, we prayerfully look to

Jesus, who can do far more than removing specks—the one who can even open the eyes of the blind.

KEY PRINCIPLES

▲ We are not surprised, because of the Fall, that these topics will be personal for our children. We can remain calm and confident that no experience our children may have automatically defines them; Jesus Christ is always able to redeem and save.

‿ Revisionist Christianity is popular, enticing, and deadly; if our children embrace it, our role is to call them out, by the grace and truth of Christ, using Scripture.

PRACTICES FOR PARENTING

● If your younger children ask about whether they are gay or trans, calmly find out more information using phrases like "Tell me what is making you wonder that."

 – You may discover that they have a simple misconception that can be cleared up by returning to God's positive vision.

 – Or you may discover that they are troubled by a feeling that they have. This is an opportunity to thank them for sharing and to assure them that no matter what they feel, you love them, God loves them, and they will have support.

▣ If your older child comes out, thank them for sharing with you and reiterate your deep love for them. Ask them questions like "How long have you noticed this experience?" "What have you felt as you related this experience to what you heard from us about sexuality?" and, if your child is a disciple, "How has it been for you in considering how to relate these feelings to your walk with Jesus?"

▲ Become familiar with the arguments for revisionist positions. Remember that the most important tool we have for discerning the truth is the word of God, and return to Scripture often, in prayer.

CONCLUSION

I HOPE YOU COME to the end of this book a little bit frustrated.

After all, how could any treatment of a topic this complex tell you exactly how to speak to and guide your specific children, in your specific neighborhood, at this specific moment in time? I expect you feel an itch remaining to be scratched from the many questions that were not answered.

This itch is also an opportunity. What I've tried to supply you with in these few pages are principles for guiding you. We saw that God's vision for our bodies and relationships really is good news and that we can talk calmly and confidently about it with even our young kids. We also saw that brokenness and sin have touched all of us and how that really impacts how we think and talk about LGBT+ questions. Finally, we looked at giving our kids the tools to relate well to those who take a different view than that of Christians and at equipping them if they choose to walk with Jesus, to do that with his grace and truth in their generation.

With these principles in mind, I hope you are better equipped to consider what parenting will look like in practice for your individual children in your specific location. Children in the suburbs of London might need a very different application of these principles than those in rural Arkansas. And the needs of your toddlers are significantly different than the needs of your teens; the needs of your intent question-askers are different than the needs of your kids who seem oblivious. As you pray and speak with others who love Jesus and care about discipling children, the Lord will lead you as you seek to apply these principles in your specific circumstances.

This is why we desperately need God's word, God's Spirit, and God's people. Your church is the place in which to satisfy that itch that needs scratching. If there are parents of your age, gather together to think and pray about how to best do this in your community. You may find that you all have a different angle, and it's important to learn from each other without pride or despair. We're all just beginning to figure it out, after all. This is why it's also important to lean on older parents in your congregation too; they may have raised their kids in a different generation, but they will have precious wisdom to share regarding how to raise children in the grace and truth of Jesus. And it's not just about connecting to older people yourself. Consider how to get your kids plugged in with their church peers; foster these relationships, as your kids need more than just you to invest in them. More than anything, pray for God's help and wisdom, and eagerly read the word in community, knowing that apart from Jesus, we can do nothing (John 15:5).

Most of all, I hope that marinating in the principles of this book has grounded your heart in faith in our loving God. He is not surprised by this moment, nor is he afraid. He knows that his gospel is the good news of salvation for all people. The death and resurrection of Jesus Christ secured victory and hope, which the Holy Spirit is working through the church even now. It is natural to fear when things are scary, but because of our relationship with the all-powerful, loving, and living true God, we can move from parenting out of fear towards parenting in secure trust in the one who will never leave us nor forsake us.

Rooted firmly in Christ Jesus, may you pray, plan, and parent by the power of the Holy Spirit, in the community of local disciples, to the glory of God the Father.

MORE FROM
RACHEL GILSON

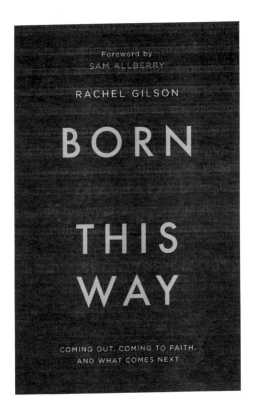

A rich portrayal of living a fulfilling life as same-sex attracted Christian while being faithful to the Bible's teaching on sexuality.

MORE ON THIS SUBJECT

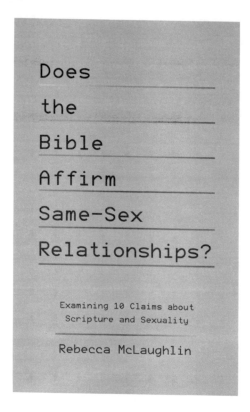

Does
the
Bible
Affirm
Same-Sex
Relationships?

Examining 10 Claims about
Scripture and Sexuality

Rebecca McLaughlin

Examines the arguments used to claim that the Bible
affirms same-sex relationships.

MORE ON THIS SUBJECT

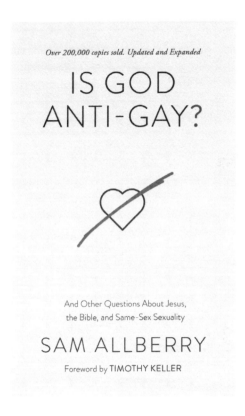

Over 200,000 copies sold. Updated and Expanded

IS GOD ANTI-GAY?

And Other Questions About Jesus,
the Bible, and Same-Sex Sexuality

SAM ALLBERRY

Foreword by TIMOTHY KELLER

A sensitive exploration of Jesus' teaching on sexuality showing how the gospel is good news for everyone, whatever their sexual orientation.